The Complete Soul
Exposing the Myth of Soul Evolution

J Douglas Bottorff

Cover Photo courtesy of USDA NRCS

ISBN: 1517219159
ISBN-13: 978-1517219154

DEDICATION

To H. Emilie Cady
Whose encouragement to go alone, think alone and seek light alone
has proven to be the most spiritually sound, life-enhancing bit of
advice I have ever received.

CONTENTS

ACKNOWLEDGMENTS

Special thanks to Anita Feuker for the time she spent reviewing this project.

.

INTRODUCTION

I started this current work originally as a revision of my first book, *A Practical Guide to Meditation and Prayer.*[1] That book went through three cover changes and six editions, none revised. Though I still agree with much of what I believed those many years ago, my understanding and my confidence as a writer has changed. About thirty pages into the revision I began to realize I would essentially be writing a whole new book. Rather than attempt a good remodel—which no doubt could be done—I decided to start fresh with a whole new building. Readers familiar with the original will recognize some of the same ideas are carried through this work.

The four nonfiction books I have written thus far represent an evolution of my thinking on spiritual matters. When *A Practical Guide to Prosperous Living* went out of print, I took the remodel route and self-published it. In the revised edition you will see the seeds of my third book, Native Soul, in their early sprouting. In this present work, these sprouts have grown into a fuller plant. I am reluctant to claim the plant is now fully mature, for I have discovered the simplest truth can remain veiled in plain sight, and I am not immune to overlooking it. Only a slight shift in perception allows us to see it, but our chest of treasured preconceptions sometimes keeps us from doing that very thing.

Though it is important to keep an open mind to the ideas of others, the standard I now value most is the one that encourages

---

[1] Unity House. 1990

me to believe in and pursue to their logical conclusions those ideas that are born in me. Emilie Cady seemed to be speaking directly to me when she wrote,

> "Each man must sooner or later learn to stand alone with his God; nothing else avails. Nothing else will ever make you master of your own destiny."

In this present work, *The Complete Soul, Exposing the Myth of Soul Evolution*, I have granted myself permission to "stand alone" with my God, to take a step outside of some of the basic givens of my formal, Unity training, while remaining solidly grounded in the principle of oneness with God.

Even though I have devoted my life to teaching the Unity message, I am not writing this book as a representative of the Unity Movement. Students of all branches of Christian New Thought should benefit from this work, but many of the insights and definitions of terms shared within these pages do not match the standard nomenclature found in the literature of this genre. This departure will be particularly noticed by those Unity students familiar with Charles Fillmore's teaching on *regeneration*. This concept, central to Fillmore's understanding and approach to the problem of the human condition, embraces soul evolution as a needed component of his supporting logic. In some cases, I make this departure in terminology for clarity, but my main intention in all cases is to suggest new ways of thinking about some widely accepted ideas and attitudes. The advice I would offer in reading this book is the same that Emilie Cady offered in her book, *Lessons In Truth:*

> In entering upon this course of instruction, each of you should, so far as possible, lay aside, for the time being, all previous theories and beliefs. By so doing you will be saved the trouble of trying, all the way through the course, to put new wine into old wineskins. If there is anything, as we proceed, which you do not understand or agree with, just let it lie passively in your mind until you have read the entire book, for many statements that would at first arouse antagonism and discussion will be clear and easily accepted a little farther on. After the course is completed, if you wish to return to your

old beliefs and ways of living, you are at perfect liberty to do so.

Think of the first nine chapters as a presentation of these changes in my thinking, why I believe they are important, and how I believe they have influenced our classic, metaphysical understanding. The last three chapters include techniques to implement the model presented. Each chapter can be summarized as follows:

Chapter 1: My Own Journey describes some personal history and key factors leading to changes in my present thinking.

Chapter 2: The Fillmorian Influence details the origins of my own exposure to the notion of soul evolution and contrasts this widely accepted concept with some of the revelations coming from the burgeoning field of near-death research.

Chapter 3: The Jesus Factor removes Jesus from the role of larger-than-life, fully regenerated Way Shower, and places him in the more accessible position of one who was aware of his complete soul and advised his listeners that they shared the same status.

Chapter 4: Consciousness, Soul, Self-Image takes a new look at the traditional *spirit, soul, and body* model of the human being and explains why *soul, consciousness, and body* provides a better way to understand the soul's present completeness and relationship to the material plane. For reasons I will make clear, I have adopted *self-image* rather than *ego* to describe the senses-based identity that most have mistaken for their real self.

Chapter 5: The Myth of Soul Evolution focuses on the soul as complete now and why embracing this truth will have a positive and productive impact on our life. I propose that we are not here because our soul has more to learn from life in a body, but simply because we have made the choice to be here.

Chapter 6: Exploring the Myth considers the undeniable facts of biological evolution, and explains why we cannot apply these facts to the soul.

Chapter 7: A Paradigm Shift demonstrates how the views we hold of the nature of God, the nature of the individual, and the nature of the individual's relationship to God are key to understanding why we, and others, hold our particular worldview.

Chapter 8: Our Executive Faculties examines our natural faculties of *imagination, faith, judgment, will,* and *elimination* and explains the role each one plays in the formation of our consciousness and life conditions.

Chapter 9: Natural Supply acknowledges the soul's spiritual support system and suggests ways of tapping into it to create the best avenue of expression in our material environment.

Chapter 10: Meditation focuses on why a first-hand experience with our soul is critical to our spiritual understanding.

Chapter 11: Meditation Exercises presents a series of exercises that range from simple contemplation to full-blown meditation practices. The exercises will help the reader overcome specific preconceptions that block a more fulfilling meditative experience.

Chapter 12: Prayer describes applications of our executive faculties to engage in a prayer technique that is simple to understand and applicable to every situation.

I consider it a privilege to present you with these thoughts. It is my desire that they stimulate new levels of self-understanding and encouragement to stand alone with your God, and to know yourself as the complete soul, not that you will one day become, but that you are right now.

CHAPTER 1

MY OWN JOURNEY

"One drop of water taken from the ocean is just as perfect ocean water as the whole great body. The constituent elements of water are exactly the same, and they are combined in precisely the same ratio or perfect relation to each other, whether we consider one drop, a pail full, a barrel full, or the entire ocean out of which the lesser quantities are taken; each is complete in itself; they differ only in quantity or degree. Each contains the whole; and yet no one would make the mistake of supposing from this statement that each drop is the entire ocean." —Emilie Cady

I was sixteen when I first read Cady's analogy. On that day, a light came on that has never gone off. She helped me understand that my spiritual essence, like water taken from the ocean, could be the same as the water in the ocean itself. I understood that I was not the *whole* of God, but I was beginning to make that all-important connection of oneness between God and myself.

Jesus, on the other hand, posed a different challenge. I understood how he, with a perfectly clear conscience, could shock his listeners with the highly charged claim that if they had known him, they had known the Father.[2] I grasped how he could be in the

Father and the Father in him, but the Father was greater.[3] If the water in the pail could speak of the ocean, could it not make the same statement? I could believe Jesus himself when he said the works he did, others could do as well, and even greater works.[4]

The issue I had was not in the claims Jesus made for himself and others. My growing discomfort was with those claims others made about him. I understood the logic of using Jesus as our primary example, our Wayshower, a clear illustration of what we can and must become. In him, we had a trustworthy standard of morality, sound spiritual logic by which we could measure and be measured. What would this very old, highly evolved soul have to say about our handling of that difficult neighbor, or that church dispute, or that beggar on the street? What would he think, say, and do if he were in our place? More importantly, what should I think, say, and do to become more like this worker of miracles who healed the sick, fed the multitudes, forgave his enemies, walked on water, calmed angry seas, and transformed his own dead flesh into shining immortality?

Where did this view of our Wayshower come from? Was Jesus really all of these things, or could this super-human portrayal simply represent a composite of old world Christian evangelicals and over-zealous modern metaphysicians? Wherever it came from, I was beginning to realize that this larger-than-life status assigned to him was completely inaccessible. If we are to believe testimony from the Gospels themselves, the most enthusiastic response to Jesus and his teachings came from the common people. Is it not possible that this Wayshower had a more down to earth understanding of our spiritual objectives?

I had no reason to doubt my spiritual teacher's portrayal of Jesus as the prime example for the rest of us still struggling to master the tyrannical desires of body and mind.[5] I could accept in theory that my essence was the same as his, that every spiritual lesson learned, every obstacle overcome added more drops to my pail. Still, Jesus and I remained light-years apart. He was not merely in another league; he was in a league of his own.

At times, I seemed to be making spiritual progress. Other times,

---

[2] John. 14:7
[3] John 10:38
[4] John 14:12
[5] Ephesians 2:3

I felt as if mine was a leaking pail, a broken cistern, as Jeremiah put it, that could hold no water.[6] Overall, I moved forward with the faith that, despite this vast gulf between where I was and where I needed to be, I was making a net gain. My evolving soul, though advancing at a glacial pace, was indeed edging forward. Even with that little voice from somewhere in the back seat of my mind constantly asking, "Are we there yet?" I continued plodding away knowing that this sense of urgency would one day be satisfied. If God was in no hurry, why should I be?

Yet this little voice would not be silenced. It did not grow quieter but louder, asking other questions that a mere further mustering of more patience would not appease. I seemed to find significant challenges to the evolving soul model from Jesus himself. In one very short parable he explained that the kingdom of heaven was like a treasure hidden in a field. A man happened by, discovered the treasure, covered it again, and in his joy sold everything he owned to buy that field.[7] The man's ability to purchase it did not hinge on a preordained time-line that evolving souls must follow. The speed by which he acquired that field depended only on his willingness to let go of his present possessions.

In my first book, *A Practical Guide to Meditation and Prayer*, I related this parable to my own spiritual awakening:

> One of the turning points in my spiritual career came during a time of deep frustration. I remember waking up one morning feeling spiritually empty (as I had for some time), so I picked up a book by Charles Fillmore and began to read. Beautiful as the words on those pages were, their effect was mocking and antagonizing instead of uplifting. I wanted to be what those words described but it seemed the harder I tried the emptier I felt inside. In a moment of anger, I threw the book down and said to God, "If You want me to learn all this stuff, then You're going to have to show me, because I'm tired of trying to do it all myself!"

> There was no reply. All day I felt mad at God for giving me a vision that seemed impossible to reach. That night I was

---

getting ready for bed and a strange thing happened. I was sitting on the edge of the bed when something in my mind suddenly opened and I could perceive a grand scheme. Everything was beautiful and in its proper place. Deep waves of love and the feeling of total acceptance rushed through me. I felt a level of contentment with myself and my surroundings that I have never felt. I could see the infinite nature of all things, animate and inanimate and it was wondrous. A knowing came to me that said, "Do not be concerned about your life, for there is a plan for you." I felt this message was not to me alone but to all who could receive it. In tears and total release I whispered, "Let it be that others can see what I am seeing now."

With such an incredibly high experience and the numerous *aftershocks* that followed, it was inconceivable that I would ever leave the beauty of this absolute love and step again into the shallow domain of illusion and half-truths generated by the senses. Yet the world called and the dazzle of illumination grew dim. This was the disappointment of waking from a satisfying dream to a hot, humid night, the lonely chirp of a cricket the stark reminder of my attachment to mundane existence.

The experience left me with the impractical knowledge that the thing everyone is looking for in churches, careers, relationships, money, power, books, sex, drugs, food, sports, movies, and countless other places, I had found in those few spiritually lucid moments. My restless self had briefly settled in peaceful repose on its eternal foundation.

In the years that followed, however, I often felt that revelation was more a curse than a blessing. It set me apart, instilled a kind of aloneness that made me question if I really belonged on this planet. I'd stumbled on the hidden treasure, but I did not want to lay it back in the ground, cover it, or go and sell all other possessions to buy the field. I wanted to lift it from the earth and hold it forever, a response that I am sure would be normal to anyone. I was the near-death experiencer who did not want to return to the body but was told, "It's not your time. You have to go back." The kingdom I had briefly experienced was not of this world. I had peered through a hole in the fence of a gated community I could not enter. Having seen this great wealth and beauty, returning to the plain streets of my world was enormously frustrating.

These few moments of lifting the veil and experiencing a profoundly beautiful cosmic awareness ultimately set me on the path to ministry. My message, fueled only by my experience of God, would center on God as a living presence whose existence I could not deny. Never in my young life had I felt so complete or so supported by the everlasting arms[8] of love that sustained my very existence, all without condition or price. I had no major healing to talk about, no rags-to-riches story I could hold out to the world as proof of my life-altering revelation. Despite this handicap, I could not deny the permanent impact this elusive treasure had on me. I knew my highest service would be that of telling others they too had their own inner field, their own hidden treasure. I took the formal steps of entering the Unity ministry to become a champion of those who, like me, had been called from that far country of life-at-the-surface and were making their way back to their true spiritual home.

For much of my ministerial career, I maintained the evolving soul model as the most workable and practical. I wandered in and out of the awareness of absolute love, sometimes feeling very much at home in God, and other times out again on yet another hopeful venture into some new far country. Why not just stay home? Why repeat this prodigal eating of husks when I knew the advantages of staying home? Why, like Paul, do I "… *not do what I want, but I do the very thing I hate?*"[9]

The best answer seemed to be the partially filled pail theory, the notion of the evolving soul. Though I was beginning to regard this idea with increasing skepticism, my pail was obviously not full. Mine was an immature soul, an adolescent doing what adolescents do. I was leaving home in high moments of strength and self-assurance, and returning when that strength waned, and fear and insecurity drove me into repentant humility. I could envision a day of coming home and staying home, but apparently I was not spiritually mature enough to settle into my true, God-given estate. I was an evolving though impatient soul not yet seasoned with the sweet stability of maturity.

Still, I could not forget the sheer completeness I had felt in

[8] Deuteronomy 33:27
[9] Romans 7:15

those fleeting moments of absolute knowing. There was no question that the water in my pail was drawn from that cosmic ocean we call God. I could not shake the growing suspicion that my pail was already full.

The Complete Soul

Then, a slight shift in my understanding of the hidden treasure occurred to me. My wife and I were relaxing at a friend's cabin in Colorado when it suddenly dawned on me that the treasure was not a partially filled pail, a potential to be developed, but one whose current value exceeded all else the man owned. I realized that this parable was a metaphor depicting the soul (hidden treasure) whose full value is already established.

I had thought of myself as having repeatedly left this field because I was spiritually immature. But the man did not leave for this reason. Quite the opposite, he left because he was mature enough to recognize the value of the treasure. Like me, he had found what he was looking for. He had stopped trying to acquire more things and was divesting himself of everything that was of lesser value than this treasure. I realized this was exactly what I was doing. My eye had become single, my choice between God and mammon clear. I wasn't leaving the field, as I supposed, for the adolescent purpose of squandering or acquiring something more. Like the man, I left to unburden myself of things of lesser value, that I may buy that field. In my own way, I was moving my self-awareness from a pail-centered self-image to its true ocean-water foundation, the soul.

The revelation did not stop there. I began to realize that if you draw one pail of water from the ocean today and another in a year from now, the age of the water in each pail is still the same. Likewise, one soul, regardless of when or how many times it has incarnated, is no more advanced than another. As with the water in the pail, the clock we think is ticking in regard to the soul is relative only to time spent in a body. The soul, like water, neither ages nor matures.

What I had gradually begun to suspect was now blossoming into a full-blown realization: The premise of an evolving soul, as logical as it seemed at one point in my understanding, was wrong. I could now see the soul is complete, has always been complete, and years devoted to further spiritual study would make it no more complete. The spiritual problem that confronts us is not the result of soul immaturity. The problem lies in what we mean when we speak the pronoun *I*. Thus far, we have associated it almost exclusively with the pail, the self-image. The *I* must be understood as a reference to the water, the soul.

My pail, I began to realize, is indeed full, my soul eternally complete. As an individualized projection of God, created in the image and after the likeness of God, it cannot be otherwise. My essence, my foundation of being is as equal in composition to God as the composition of the water in the pail is equal to that of the ocean. As Jesus put it, the harvest (soul completion) is not four months,[10] four lifetimes, or four-hundred lifetimes away. This field is already ripe for harvest. Everything is in place right now. The truth that sets us free is present, accessible, and will never be more so than it is at this moment.

I was beginning to see that from the instant I stumbled upon my own treasure, I had been undergoing a major shift in values. I was not aware of it at the time, but I had begun selling those possessions that were preventing me from embracing the truth of my soul. Though I am still sorting through inconsistencies in self-perceptions and beliefs about the world, I have come to accept that we are not here to convince the world we are something other than that which we are at our sincerest, most authentic level. If we express qualities the world deems great, it is not because we have labored hard to manufacture these. We express them because we are simply doing what comes most natural. We made the choice to be here, to give expression to our soul, to give it a face, a voice, and a way to interact in the world that is ours and ours alone.

This is why, in this book, I am placing emphasis on experiencing the soul rather than knowing God. It's not that knowing God is unimportant, but I choose to follow Jesus' premise that if you have known me [the soul], you have known the Father [the soul's source]. Studying a single pail of ocean water is not nearly as intimidating as studying the entire ocean. Yet following this analogy, understanding of the composition of the water in the pail is equivalent to understanding the composition of the water in the entire ocean. When you experience your soul, you experience God.

---

[10] John 4:35

All of us carry preconceived ideas about who and what we are at the spiritual level. Because I attribute much of my early understanding of this subject to the writings of Charles Fillmore, I think it's appropriate to examine this influence and to show how and why I have reconsidered its place of importance in my current thinking.

CHAPTER 2

THE FILLMORIAN INFLUENCE

And when he entered the temple, the chief priests and the elders of the people came up to him as he was teaching, and said, "By what authority are you doing these things, and who gave you this authority?"[11]

Though my first exposure to Unity was through the writings of Emilie Cady, I would discover later that she wrote as a representative of the Unity Movement, co-founded by Charles and Myrtle Fillmore. Prior to this discovery, I had no knowledge of Unity as an organization.

Cady's book, *Lessons in Truth*, first appeared as a series of articles in *Unity*. This series was the Fillmore's response to a *Unity* subscriber's request to *"...have one of your clearest writers, one who understands the principles, and the uninformed mind of a student, write an explanation of this grand Truth in very simple form and in simple, clear words."* As a regular contributor to a number of Unity publications, the Fillmores selected Cady for the task. In my opinion, her work still represents the gold standard of presentations of Unity's core teachings.

---

[11] Matthew 21:23

In the meantime, Fillmore continued developing his own writing skills, and deepening his understanding of spiritual principles. In much the same way science has been on a quest for the *theory of everything* (a single theory linking all aspects of the material universe), so Fillmore was in search of a spiritual key for resolving the full range of human problems. Having explored many of the world's religious and occult teachings, he narrowed his search to the example and teachings of Jesus Christ. There he found his *theory of everything*, his universal key that, in his view, held the promise of ending all human suffering. This key was his concept of *regeneration*, which he defined as:

> "A change in which abundant spiritual life, even eternal life, is incorporated into the body. The transformation that takes place through bringing all the forces of mind and body to the support of the Christ ideal. The unification of Spirit, soul, and body in spiritual oneness."[12]

Once it solidified in his own thinking, this concept provided the logic that inspired Fillmore's elaborate vision of humankind's ultimate goal, a snapshot of which we find in the opening paragraph of his book, *The Twelve Powers of Man*:

> "Jesus prophesied the advent of a race of men who would sit with Him on twelve thrones, judging the twelve tribes of Israel. This book explains the meaning of this mystical reference, what and where the twelve thrones are, and what attainments are necessary by man before he can follow Jesus in this phase of his regeneration. Regeneration follows generation in the development of man. Generation sustains and perpetuates the human; regeneration unfolds and glorifies the divine."[13]

The scriptural support for this lofty vision comes from the King James Version (KJV) of the Gospel of Matthew. Jesus and his disciples are in conversation, with the disciples expressing their concern of having given up everything to follow Jesus. What rewards await them?

[12] Fillmore, Charles. *The Revealing Word*. Unity Books
[13] Twelve Powers of Man. Charles Fillmore. Unity Books

And Jesus said unto them, Verily I say unto you, That ye which have followed me, in the *regeneration* when the Son of man shall sit in the throne of his glory, ye also shall sit upon twelve thrones, judging the twelve tribes of Israel.[14]

Given the fact that he makes this text and the concept of regeneration the central theme of his teaching, his theory of everything, scholars today would find Fillmore's interpretation of the above scripture problematic. In the entire Bible, there are but two occurrences of the word, *regeneration* (Matthew 19:28, Titus 3:5). As we've seen, the Matthew reference appears only in the KJV.[15] Modern translations drop *regeneration* from Matthew, favoring instead phrases like "*in the new world*"[16] and "*at the renewal of all things.*"[17]

That the followers of the Jesus movement would have seen this passage as a mystical reference to body and soul regeneration is doubtful. Every aspect of the Bible is, of course, fair game for metaphysical interpretation, but Matthew's passage obviously points to the literal second coming, the ushering in of the new age,[18] and the rewards for those who have sacrificed everything for their faith.

"And every one who has left houses or brothers or sisters or father or mother or children or lands, for my name's sake, will receive a hundredfold, and inherit eternal life."[19]

As one trained in the foundation principles of Unity, I attribute my early understanding of the soul as an evolving entity to Charles Fillmore. Though Cady certainly implied it, she was far less energetic in her discourse on the particulars of the subject. We will see in the remainder of this chapter that Fillmore presented Jesus as the sole example of the highly evolved, spiritually unified, completely regenerated human being. Based on my respect for Fillmorian authority, this is the view I endorsed before I had the

---

[14] Matthew 19:28 KJV
[15] King James Version was published in 1612
[16] Revised Standard Version. 1946-1957
[17] New Revised Standard Version. 1989
[18] Mark 10:30, Luke 18:30
[19] Matthew 19:29

confidence to draw my own conclusions. Presenting the reasons why I have now come to a different understanding of the soul and of Jesus and his role is the subject of this chapter and the one that follows.

From the writers of the New Testament to now, all generations of Christian leaders have utilized the words and actions of Jesus to lend authority and credibility to the advancement of their organizational causes and personal agendas. There was much tension between Paul and his appeal to embrace the Gentiles, and those who sought to limit passing the message of Jesus exclusively to the Jewish community. Using Jesus and his messianic credentials as their authority, each side accused the other of preaching a false gospel.

Some years ago, a couple asked me to perform a wedding in a well-known chapel in the foothills near Denver. When the Evangelical Christian owners of the chapel learned that I was a Unity minister, they barred me from performing the ceremony. They said Unity was "theologically impure" and, therefore, non-Christian.

It was attitudes like these that I believe motivated Fillmore to go to extreme lengths to not only prove Unity was theologically pure, but to show it was the purest and truest representation of the Christian message. "*We believe all the doctrines of Christianity spiritually interpreted*"[20] He applied his interpretation of Jesus, a mighty, larger-than-life, fully regenerated *type-man*, very much alive and standing at the head of the Unity movement, as the primary means of advancing his system of thought. He insisted that long established ideas about Jesus did not go far enough, that Jesus was all they said and so much more. He was the ultimate Wayshower of the human race, the great example of what the fully regenerated human being was to look like.

This portrayal, like those of his more traditional counterparts, set an idealized standard of spiritual and physical accomplishment that, in my observation, has driven some, including Fillmore himself, to obsess over unrealistic expectations of the body. In an article written in 1920 he wrote,

---

[20] #31, Unity's Statement of Faith

"The Spirit showed me several years ago that I must quit having my picture taken; that I must quit looking into the mirror and seeing myself as a murky imagination had formed me. I had within me the concept of a fine looking young man, but when I looked into the glass, or when I had my picture taken, he did not appear. And other people did not see him and they began to impress me with error both within and without."[21]

Though the legends persist that Fillmore, through vigorous affirmative prayer work, did manage to regain some of his youthful appearance, an outside observer saw him at age 84 as a "white-haired man" bearing the same failing physical and mental characteristics typical of that age. According to Myrtle, he became reluctant to appear in public *"until he has completed his demonstration of healing his leg,"*[22] the result of a childhood injury that plagued him his entire life. Showing any signs of age or illness would have run counter to his declaration that the human being was capable of living in the body forever. Asked if he expected to live forever in his body, Fillmore responded in this way:

"This question is often asked by Unity readers. Some of them seem to think that I am either a fanatic or a joker if I take myself seriously in the hope that I shall with Jesus attain eternal life in the body. But the fact is that I am very serious about the matter."[23]

Though he did not succeed, there is no doubt that he was committed to the idea. The force with which he advanced his ideal influenced many Unity followers to adopt this type-man he saw in Jesus as the Holy Grail of spiritual attainment. One woman I knew, steeped in Fillmore's denial of old age, was adamant about not speaking her age, believing that acknowledging it would make it so. I am certain that any stranger meeting her at any point in her life would have been able to guess her age based on her bodily appearance. To many who knew her, including myself, this all

---

[21] Quotation taken from, The Spiritual Journey of Charles Fillmore. Neal Vahle. Templeton Foundation Press. 2008

[22] Ibid.

[23] Ibid.

seemed an overly dramatic game.

I support much of what Charles Fillmore taught and I encourage all to read the full body of his works. But I have never been able to accept his ideas on the potential for physical immortality, or that Jesus pioneered and advocated eternal life in the physical body. My sense is that Fillmore's life-long struggle with his own physical condition is the thing that made soul and body regeneration his personal focus.

Soul Evolution and Reincarnation

This glorified portrayal of Jesus, put forward as our ultimate example of spiritual achievement, has forced us to accept that the soul of the average person, far from hitting this extraordinarily high mark, must be evolving toward the perfection of Christ Consciousness. Fillmore taught that all people could eventually reach this level, making it necessary to include the concepts of soul evolution and reincarnation as bridging mechanisms needed to carry out this lofty achievement.

He was not alone in adopting soul evolution as the means of facilitating the individual's march toward spiritual perfection, but Fillmore was especially emphatic in tying soul development directly to the condition of the physical body. He saw the body as *"the highest-formed manifestation of creative Mind, and that it is capable of unlimited expression of that Mind."* As we have seen, this unlimited expression would ultimately translate into physical immortality.

> "When man realizes that there is but one body-idea and that the conditions in his body express the character of his thought, he has the key to bodily perfection and immortality in the flesh."[24]

The body, according to Fillmore, projects the condition of the soul. The degeneration of the body, through aging and death, indicates the soul has not yet evolved to full alignment with the Christ ideal that rests in the mind of God.

> "If you believe in old age and bodily decrepitude and decay, you will find that all the little cells throughout your organism

---

[24] Fillmore, Charles. *Christian Healing*. Unity Books

are carrying in their depths just such pictures, as the clear waters of the lake reflect the trees and the clouds."[25]

The body, then, is a kind of barometer that reflects the state of the soul. The aging process and any separation of spirit, soul, and body brought on by physical death are due to a *"transgression of the divine law."*[26] According to this view, the soul contains many ideas that are not in alignment with what is true of Spirit. Because Fillmore believed the "soul makes the body," the body displays, in the form of disease and death, the untruths held at the soul level. The remedy is to regenerate the soul, bringing its sum of ideas up to the standard of the *I Am*, the support of the Christ ideal. In the meantime, the soul is in a constant state of evolving from a mortal to an immortal condition, which the body follows.

As I've pointed out, this evolution of soul and body takes place through multiple incarnations. This belief, perhaps inadvertently, elevates reincarnation to the status of an *evolutionary requirement* or, as Fillmore calls it:

"... a merciful provision of our loving Father to the end that all may have opportunity to attain immortality through regeneration, as did Jesus."[27]

In other words, Fillmore does not present reincarnation as a choice-based option, but instead makes it an evolutionary inevitability, a required link in his chain of logic. In addition to merciful, we are compelled to accept reincarnation as a necessary provision of our soul's continued progress, and we are forced to measure this progress by the present condition of our physical body.

I believe it is an unnecessary burden to think the body and its present condition represent the condition of the soul. According to this association, if the body is expressing disease and limitation of any kind, it is because a similar condition exists in the soul. This problem is the result of considering the terms *soul* and *consciousness* as having the same meaning. We'll take an in-depth, alternative

---

[25] Fillmore, Charles. *Talks on Truth.* Unity Books
[26] #21, Unity's Statement of Faith

[27] # 22, ibid

look at the terms, *soul, consciousness,* and *self-image* in Chapter 4.

The health of our body, or the lack thereof, does indeed have a direct relation to the instabilities and stresses brought on by our consciousness. This is very different from suggesting the soul is flawed and these flaws are out-picturing in the body. The beliefs generated by the self-image act as a kind of weather system containing clouds that mask the sunlight of the soul. The soul's radiance is perpetual, but the self-image produces a cloud cover of fear and stress that has a negative impact on our mental and physical well-being. We know that a person can display a perfectly healthy body and remain spiritually asleep. Likewise, one can be spiritually awake and still be afflicted with a physical malady or handicap.

Jesus and Soul Evolution

We can trace the association of soul evolution and reincarnation far back into the history of Eastern religions. The idea of the soul being reborn in another body as a further chance to attain higher consciousness, or to work out one's karma, is a central tenet. Fillmore put a Christianized spin on this process by declaring Jesus the only person who had ever lifted his physical body to this fully regenerated condition. Through *"conscious union with Jesus in the regeneration,"* he wrote, each person could *"transform his body and make it perpetually healthy, therefore immortal, and that he can attain eternal life in this way and in no other way."*[28] Jesus *"was the 'first-fruits' of those who are coming out of the mortal into the immortal."* According to the logic of these statements, one not only had to be Christian to gain eternal life, he or she had to be a *metaphysical* Christian.

This view of reincarnation explains why, with the exception of the ascended Jesus, we see no fully regenerated humans roaming planet earth.

> "He [Jesus] was the type man, the Way-Shower, and, through following His example and taking on His character as a spiritual-minded man, we shall come into the same consciousness."[29]

To Fillmore, physical death, which he described as the *"terror of*

---

[28] #19, ibid
[29] Fillmore, Charles. *Twelve Powers of Man.* Unity Books

humanity," represents a complete breakdown in adherence to the law of regeneration.

At the point of physical death, Fillmore envisioned the soul entering a kind of sleep in which neither learning nor advancement of any kind took place. It is with the next physical incarnation that the soul resumes its evolutionary journey from where it left off in the previous incarnation.

> "As death has no power to help anyone, the condition of the Adam man is not bettered by dying. Therefore, when people are re-embodied they 'come forth . . . unto the resurrection of damnation,' in other words, condemnation or correction. Everyone begins where he left off."[30]

This assertion clearly runs counter to the findings of researchers in the field of near-death studies, research that was unavailable in Fillmore's time. Far from slipping into sleep or a coma, the majority of near-death experiencers report that they feel more alive than ever. A substantial number report tapping a universal wisdom and love beyond anything they can describe. They often see through the shallow interests and cares of their worldly pursuits. It is common for those devoted to chasing materialistic ends to lift their standards and aim for higher purposes. Atheists return believing in God. Religious believers have their minds opened far beyond the dogmatic parameters of their training. Virtually none of them "begins where he left off," even when their episodes last but a few minutes. As researchers have discovered, the near-death experience often changes people to their core, and in moments. This is a sharp contrast to the view expressed by Fillmore:

> "Awakening cannot be associated with dying. The idea that man awakens to spiritual or any kind of consciousness immediately after "death," whether in heaven, hell, purgatory, or elsewhere, is opposed to Truth. His awakening must take place here, during the time of "life," at least while he is partially awake and before he sinks into that deeper sleep or coma that we call death."[31]

---

[30] Fillmore, Charles. *Keep a True Lent.* Unity Books
[31] Fillmore, Charles. *Mysteries of Genesis.* Unity Books

Viewing physical death as he did, can we wonder that Fillmore failed to see any kind of spiritual value associated with the loss of the body? The evidence is now overwhelming that so-called death is neither a deeper sleep nor a coma, but a state of enhanced lucidity. In this state, the individual is more alive and alert, their ability to see, hear, and know more acute than at any time while in the body. In light of what we are learning from this research, the argument can and should be made that overcoming death has less to do with physical immortality and more to do with the revelation that there is, in fact, no death. *"Death,"* as one NDEr concluded, *"is a really nasty lie."*

Carl Jung Testimony

There are some who pass off near-death research as merely anecdotal and, therefore, inconsequential and unreliable. The experiencer, they might say, is predisposed to a certain kind of imagery due to their beliefs. This may be true to some extent, but we cannot ignore the fact that there are common elements found in the overwhelming majority of cases from all cultures and demographics. Nor can we ignore the testimony of individuals we consider highly credible, especially when they gave it prior to the popularization of near-death studies.

One notable case is that of Swiss psychiatrist, Carl Jung. After having a heart attack accompanied by an NDE, he wrote:

> "I would never have imagined that any such experience was possible. It was not a product of imagination. The visions and experiences were utterly real; there was nothing subjective about them; they all had a quality of absolute objectivity."[32]

So real was this experience that Jung, like many before and after him, was quite reluctant to return to the confines of his physical body.

> "In reality, a good three weeks were still to pass before I could truly make up my mind to live again. I could not eat because all food repelled me. The view of city and mountains from my sickbed seemed to me like a painted curtain with black holes

---

[32] Jung, Carl, Aniela Jaffé. 1965. *Memories, Dreams, Reflections*. Vintage, a division of Random House

in it, or a tattered sheet of newspaper full of photographs that meant nothing. Disappointed, I thought: "Now I must return to 'the box system' again." For it seemed to me as if behind the horizon of the cosmos a three-dimensional world had been artificially built up, in which each person sat by himself in a little box. And now I should have to convince myself all over again that this was important! Life and the whole world struck me as a prison, and it bothered me beyond measure that I should again be finding all that quite in order. I had been so glad to shed it all, and now it had come about that I—along with everyone else—would again be hung up in a box by a thread."[33]

Jung did not discount the value of the awakening he experienced during his near-death episode. Nor did he pass off the insight it provided as subjective fantasy. He treated it as a real experience that had a profound impact on his thinking. His case is important, not only for the name recognition, but also for the fact that he was a highly trained and respected observer of mental processes. Is it likely that Jung would have jeopardized his professional legacy speculating on these visions and experiences had he considered them anything but utterly real?

The Choice to Reincarnate

As I've mentioned, I like to think of reincarnation as a choice rather than as an evolutionary requirement. Seen this way, we can think of our earthly incarnation as something far more than Fillmore's resurrection of damnation. With choice as the prime factor, we can logically conclude that we will incarnate on earth as long as something here holds our interest. When events or circumstances make it unattractive—a natural global catastrophe for example—it is quite conceivable that we simply refrain from taking up a body until conditions become more to our liking. It is also reasonable to consider that we may incarnate at a particular time to advance a cause, or to help rebuild a waning human population brought on by war or natural disaster.

Around seventy thousand years ago, Toba, a super volcano in Indonesia, exploded into one of earth's largest eruptions. This

---

[33] ibid

environmental disaster triggered severe climate change and may have reduced the human population to as few as 3,000 to 10,000.[34] Is it unreasonable to assume that, given the choice, many fewer individuals would incarnate in such a compromised environment? On the other hand, some, like first responders, might relish the chance to rush in and help the human species recover.

Without going too far afield here, can we discount the possibility of multiple, biospheric environments existing throughout the universe? New studies estimate that our Milky Way galaxy alone contains 100 billion planets. If this is true and one environment does not appeal to our interests or fill a need we feel compelled to address, is it out of the range of possibility that we may simply choose another?

Charles Fillmore placed the soul in an evolving continuum from which the only escape was full regeneration of soul and body. His conclusion that only one person, Jesus, had successfully run this evolutionary gauntlet casts a dim light on the average individual's chances of a full awakening in this lifetime. That he believed absolutely in this model is shown in his advocating that an extraordinary spiritual revolution was underway:

> "Everywhere true metaphysicians are preparing themselves to be members in the great colony that Jesus is to set up, by working to eliminate from their mind all selfish ideas, along with all other discordant vibrations that produce inharmony among members of the same group."[35]

I have little doubt that he envisioned Unity Village as the beginning of this great colony of true metaphysicians. In my earlier years, I would have gladly counted myself a willing and expectant resident of this great colony. I have since concluded that the image of Jesus put forward by Charles Fillmore is the product of his own speculation. The Jesus every author presents, and I include myself, is the Jesus that would exist if our specific lines of logic were correct. I'll present my view of him in the following chapter.

---

[34] According to the genetic bottleneck theory, between 50,000 and 100,000 years ago, human populations sharply decreased to 3,000–10,000 surviving individuals. The theory is supported by genetic evidence suggesting that today's humans are descended from a very small population of between 1,000 and 10,000 breeding pairs that existed about 70,000 years ago. (Wikipedia: Genetic Bottleneck Theory).

[35] Fillmore, Charles. *Prosperity.* Unity Books

The sheer ambiguity of historical facts have made Jesus fair game for a wide range of interpretations advanced as Truth. We wind up with a blend of emotionally charged imagery mixed with a line of spiritual logic that careful scrutiny or new research will likely expose as having little or no basis in historical or scientific fact.

CHAPTER 3

THE JESUS FACTOR

My views of Jesus have changed over the years. I no longer tie his relevance to whether or not he was the miracle worker, the savior who died for my sins, or even the Wayshower who represents all that I might one day become. Through various periods I have seen him through the eyes of the traditional Christian, and I have felt remorse for his death on the cross for my sins. I have also seen him through the eyes of the metaphysical Christian, known the assurance of embracing him as Fillmore's type-man, the extraordinary example of the person I may someday become.

Despite such a wide range of experience, I made no significant progress in spiritual understanding until I followed the simple instruction of Jesus himself: to go into my inner room and pray to the Father who is in secret.[36] Drawing near the very fountainhead of my being has yielded the most productive spiritual insights. Why take the word of another when it is possible to know and experience God firsthand?

The Jesus I have come to know through my own study and meditative experience is a man who fully discovered and spoke from his soul, a fact that profoundly distinguishes him from the average person. I'm not suggesting he was different in spiritual capacity. He was different in focus and in self-understanding. We

---

[36] Matthew 6:6

have made him into something beyond the reach of the common people he addressed, and I do not believe he would have approved. *"Why do you call me good? No one is good but God alone."*[37] He demonstrated what it is to be a divinely awakened human and pointed out that the things this revelation enabled him to see and do, others could see and do as well.[38]

My change of attitude has not minimized or diminished in the least the role of Jesus as an extraordinary example of spiritual genius. The insights I now glean from many of his sayings have elevated the way I think of others and myself. These insights have caused me to consider why he seemed to have such faith in the spiritual capacity of the common person.

I have concluded that the completeness he found in himself, he also saw in others. He understood how people were blinding themselves to this inner kingdom, and he set himself to the task of encouraging them to open their spiritual eyes. I think of Jesus as one who gave voice to his soul, a voice that we intuitively recognize as it stirs our hidden depths, giving us the eyes to see and the ears to hear the message of a kindred spirit describing a spiritual geography we ourselves presently inhabit. He did not speak of one day reaching a pool of wholeness, but of today taking up our bed of appearance-inspired thinking and walking. He claimed no monopoly on Truth. The revelation of Truth, by his voice or by any voice that speaks it, is a revelation of what is true now and what has always been true of all people for all time.

The words and acts attributed to Jesus are grains of evidence, fossilized remnants if you will, that bear the characteristics of his original, inwardly oriented message. He spoke the language of the soul, the language spoken by mystics through the ages who have transcended religious boundaries. Jesus, and all mystics, have been grossly misunderstood by religious professionals.

> "The unspiritual man does not receive the gifts of the Spirit of God, for they are folly to him, and he is not able to understand them because they are spiritually discerned."[39]

Because the spiritual dimension defies description, those who

---

come to know it cannot find the language to describe the subjective nature of their experience. They have resorted to parable, metaphor, allegory, and simile. Jesus likens this heavenly kingdom to a grain of mustard seed, leaven, treasure hidden in a field, a net thrown into the sea, a householder who brings out his treasure, and so on. These remnants from Jesus' life are couched and preserved in a matrix of religious trappings that, in all likelihood, share a closer alliance to the teachings and intentions of the early church than to Jesus. Adding to this confusion, the New Testament presents a diversity of views of who Jesus was and what he represented. None of the New Testament writers wrote with the intention of having their work compiled into a single document. Luke, acknowledging a variety of versions of the story of Jesus, took it upon himself to set the record straight:

> "Inasmuch as many have undertaken to compile a narrative of the things which have been accomplished among us, just as they were delivered to us by those who from the beginning were eyewitnesses and ministers of the word, it seemed good to me also, having followed all things closely for some time past, to write an orderly account for you, most excellent Theophilus, that you may know the truth concerning the things of which you have been informed."[40]

Ignoring the independent views of each author, the traditional Christian community has drawn from this diversity of sources to create the single composite of the Jesus that has become familiar to most today. There were other views in ancient times. For example, the Gnostic Christian writings, discovered in a cave in Nag Hammadi, Egypt, in 1945, represent a very different view of Jesus. Though this fringe community embraced a theology foreign to the Christian traditionalist, I am in full agreement with their belief that you must first know yourself at the spiritual level before you can understand a man like Jesus. In *The Gospel of Thomas*, we find this intriguing observation:

> Jesus said, "If your leaders say to you, 'Look, the (Father's) kingdom is in the sky,' then the birds of the sky will precede

---

[40] Luke 1:1-4

you. If they say to you, 'It is in the sea,' then the fish will precede you. Rather, the (Father's) kingdom is within you and it is outside you. When you know yourselves, then you will be known, and you will understand that you are children of the living Father. But if you do not know yourselves, then you live in poverty, and you are the poverty."[41]

That aspect of Christian tradition that considers the individual born in sin and in need of salvation does not place a high premium on self-knowledge. Excluding emphasis on knowing one's self has led to a level of spiritual poverty unnoticed by those who measure spiritual success by denominational standards rather than by the presence of personal enlightenment. Embracing the view of Jesus transmitted by authority through the centuries requires no degree of self-knowledge. It requires only a profession of faith in the validity of the transmission.

We will not be able to prove definitively who Jesus was or know how he thought of himself. What we can do through an examination of the historical record is observe the centuries-long struggle to hammer out a singular view of Jesus from a multitude of interpretations and know from this that we are not actually seeing the man. We can take from this collective homogenizing effort the cue that allows us to venture beyond the realm of enshrined opinion, beyond the Jesus forced into the service of the professional theologian, and discover the Jesus who strikes that sympathetic chord of our soul.

Our quest for spiritual authenticity provides the heat that separates the slag of orthodoxy and tradition from the precious metal of truth, as relevant today as it was in the day of Jesus. We are left with the task of discerning between the voices of authority and that live wire of Truth that electrifies and enlightens the mystic. "*My sheep hear my voice ...*"[42] is, for me, a kind of knowing wink to those who recognize this language of the soul.

The pure voice of Jesus that I hear rising through the theological mix of the Gospels, the New Testament as a whole and views shared by the unorthodox, is a voice that resonates with my very core. I do not find a Jesus compelling me to follow him on his

---

path, but one that points out that I have my own. I hear him telling me that for this I was born, for this I have come into the world, to bear witness to the truth of my being, to walk the path that is mine alone and no one else's.

In the same way New Thought has challenged the traditional views held about Jesus, it is appropriate that we question and challenge views considered integral to New Thought logic today. I assume that Jesus encouraged his listeners to do little more than follow him in shedding the dogmatic beliefs of religious orthodoxy. I believe he encouraged people to discover for themselves the truth of their spiritual nature, which provides the strongest, most profound catalyst for change at the fundamental level of one's being.

In the next chapter, we'll revisit some key terms that I think will help bring clarity to our understanding of the soul. A new look at these terms will be helpful in further dispelling the myth of soul evolution.

CHAPTER 4

CONSCIOUSNESS, SOUL, SELF-IMAGE

My Unity training taught that the terms *soul* and *consciousness* are used interchangeably. Charles Fillmore described the soul as *"man's consciousness ... the many accumulated ideas back of his present expression."*[43] In this book, I apply this definition to the *self-image* rather than to the soul. In our general understanding of the self-image, we think of it as the many accumulated ideas that make up the person we believe we are. It's the way we think about ourselves, our abilities, our life experiences, our memories, and our physical appearance. In Walt Whitman's *Song of Myself*, he refers to that part that is *"...not contain'd between my hat and boots..."* Painting in broad strokes, we think of the self-image as that which *is* contained between the hat and boots.

In contrast, the soul is the immutable core of our being, our spiritual center that cannot be contained between the hat and the boots. The soul is eternal, unaffected by our ever-changing beliefs, moods, and the perpetually shifting sands of daily thinking. The soul is the spiritual core that we associate with the *Christ*, that image and likeness of God that is already complete, no evolution required. It is that deeper essence that survives when there is no more need for a hat and boots.

---

[43] Revealing Word

The self-image generally treats the soul as an abstraction and often confuses it with intense, sincere feeling. You have heard someone say that something touched their soul when they really mean something stirred their emotions. Many confuse the short-lived intoxicant of emotional elation with the more permanent experience of the spiritual awakening. The two are quite different.

It is true that invoking the intellectual and emotional powers available to the self-image can stir our lives in positive ways. But without incorporating an awareness of the soul as the primary influence, these changes are short-lived ripples that roll over the surface of our self-image. They do not instill the depth of spiritual understanding that is native to the soul. Without a conscious connection with the soul, our self-image continues to be plagued with the dull but incessant knowledge that something essential to our being is missing.

Understanding Consciousness

It is also important to understand the term *consciousness*, its relationship to the self-image, and the role it plays in the process of soul expression. In its common usage, we think of consciousness as awareness. If we say a person loses consciousness, we are saying they are no longer aware of themselves or their surroundings. They are unconscious.

In addition, spiritual literature treats consciousness as the *sum of an individual's belief system*. When writer Emmet Fox popularized the phrase, *life is consciousness*, he was recognizing a relationship between the beliefs we hold as true and the conditions of our lives. It is widely accepted, therefore, that if we want to better our conditions, we start, not by changing the conditions, but by changing our belief system, our consciousness. These new beliefs affect our decision-making processes, actions, and ultimately work out as new life conditions.

While consciousness, as the sum of our beliefs, does indeed influence our interaction with the world, the ideas we harbor are far from random. Just as our solar system has the sun as a center of gravity holding the planets in their orbits, so consciousness has a center of gravity that holds its many ideas in place. The makeup of our consciousness, therefore, is an *effect* of our center of gravity. This center of gravity can either be the self-image or it can be the soul. If it is the self-image, the ideas we accept as true reflect what we believe to be true of this self-image. If our center of gravity is the soul, our ideas will reflect what is true of the soul. Changing our center of gravity, then, automatically influences the composition of our consciousness.

When Jesus spoke to Nicodemus he likened this shift in the center of gravity to a new birth:

> Jesus answered him, "Truly, truly, I say to you, unless one is born anew, he cannot see the kingdom of God." Nicodemus said to him, "How can a man be born when he is old? Can he enter a second time into his mother's womb and be born?" Jesus answered, "Truly, truly, I say to you, unless one is born of water and the Spirit, he cannot enter the kingdom of God. That which is born of the flesh is flesh, and that which is born of the Spirit is spirit."[44]

To be born in this context refers to the basis from which we interpret and experience our world. To be born of the flesh is to see the world from the externally grounded, senses-based self-image. To be born of the Spirit is to identify with the true core of our being, the Spirit-sustained soul.

This shift is illustrated in the ritual of water baptism. The initiate goes into the water as one thing and comes out another. To be born of water and the Spirit, we loosen our death-grip on our seemingly precious self-image and recognize the soul as the true core of our identity.

Achieving this shift is the primary objective of meditation. We turn our attention from normal, intellectual input to an intuitive receptivity focused on the soul, a process we will explore in depth in future chapters. Using the language in the above scriptural passage, we go into meditation born of the flesh and, if we are successful making the shift, we emerge born of the Spirit.

I do not believe that Jesus was talking about a drawn-out educational process. To the contrary, the way he taught seemed to indicate a letting go rather than the acquisition of new information.

> Truly, I say to you, unless you turn and become like children, you will never enter the kingdom of heaven. Whoever

---

[44] John 3:3-6

humbles himself like this child, he is the greatest in the kingdom of heaven.[45]

It was said of Jesus himself that the Jews marveled that he had much learning yet had "never studied."[46] His learning, according to John, was imparted by the one who "sent" him, the Father, the soul who was interfacing with the world as the man Jesus.[47] His teaching, then and now, is a challenge to the academic steeped in the notion that the intellectually guided self-image is the single-most important avenue of learning.

Who You Think You Are, Who You Think You Can Be

The self-image is your self-summary that includes personality traits, physical characteristics, the sum of your life experiences, your interpretation of these experiences, and the values that you place on all of these things. In other words, the self-image is a composite of who you think you *are*, who you think you *should be* and, in your more positive moments, who you think you *can be*.

If you are dissatisfied with your current condition, you may naturally seek to move from who you think you are to who you think you should be. To do this, you may seek out a "spiritual" solution. What many call the spiritual path is little more than an intellectually construed process whose focus is the further development and improvement of the self-image. This is simply an attempt to move from who we think we are to another self-image we think we should be. What we're calling an inner journey is little more than a trip through the wilderness of spiritual preconceptions gleaned from books and lectures, and stored in the subconscious mind. We are seeking to exchange one senses-based self-image for another more advanced model, an upgraded collection of the enlightened thoughts of others. The reason we are making little or no progress is because we never leave the confines of the self-image. Changes we make in our thinking, positive as they might be, never produce the desired fulfillment that we deeply crave. The change we must make is one that shifts our center of gravity from the self-image to the soul.

---

[45] Matthew 18:3-4
[46] John 7:15
[47] John 7:16

The commonly adopted model of the individual included in my formal training is the three-fold nature of *spirit*, *soul*, and *body*. Spirit is the unchanging center, soul (consciousness) is depicted as the ever-changing, ever-evolving system of belief, and the body is the physical clothing of the soul.

To better align with our common usage of these terms today, I have adopted the model of *soul*, *consciousness*, and *body*.

As we've seen, consciousness, the ever-changing sum of our beliefs, is a kind of mental atmosphere that is held in place by the center of gravity that is our central identity. For most, this is the self-image. Our spiritual objective is not to improve the self-image but to make this center of gravity the soul instead. The central identity, whether it is the self-image or the soul, determines the composition of our consciousness, a very important idea that we'll examine in detail in a moment.

From external sources, the self-image gathers the beliefs that comprise its consciousness. It does this gathering through the senses-driven intellect, that is, from the outside in. In contrast, the soul generates and expresses the ideas that make up its consciousness intuitively, from the inside out. The soul draws its being from the infinite fountain that is God, and it expresses this inspiration to the outside world through its consciousness. Consciousness, I'll say again, can be generated either by the self-image or it can be generated by the soul. This means we are talking about two ways of learning, two distinct ways of knowing that require entirely different approaches.

Consciousness Building

Learning is the deliberate act of enhancing or changing the ideas that make up our consciousness. In spiritual terminology, we refer to this learning process as *consciousness development* or *consciousness building*. Of the two kinds of consciousness building, the most common is that employed by the self-image. This type of learning involves the development of a skill-set through study and practice. Learning to play chess involves acquiring an understanding of how you may move the pieces. Reading a simple illustrated manual on these basics can provide you with this information. Knowing how pieces may be moved is only the beginning. The chess player interested in mastering the game develops an understanding of strategy, a skill enhanced through further study and the actual playing with opponents.

Whether we are learning to play chess, drive a car, or we are studying for a career in physics, the learning process is much the same. We take on ideas and we learn to apply them in real-life situations. We have developed the consciousness for a thing when it becomes second nature to us.

Because it greatly increases our ability to get along in the world, this type of learning is the basis of our educational system. If getting along in the world is our only concern, and it *is* a concern, this type of intellectually based learning would suffice. Those who receive the spiritual nudge engage in a different kind of learning, one that requires an in-depth shift from the self-image to the soul. With this type of learning, the soul employs introspective meditation as the primary means of opening the intuitive portal, a topic we'll explore in Chapters 10 and 11. Intuitive learning is subjective, experiential in nature, and does not utilize the same intellectual processes used by the self-image. One person cannot pass spiritual enlightenment or a spiritual experience to another. One can stir the imagination and the emotion by relating their experience to others, but the experience itself cannot be transferred. Each person must have his or her own experience.

When it comes to consciousness building then, of what value is the intellect to the spiritual aspirant? Or what value is the subjective, meditative experience to that goal-driven, intellectually-oriented, practical side of us that is seeking a better life through success in a career?

Albert Einstein raised a similar question in the often-quoted statement he made concerning light, and whether it behaved as a particle or as a wave:

> "It seems as though we must use sometimes the one theory and sometimes the other, while at times we may use either. We are faced with a new kind of difficulty. We have two contradictory pictures of reality; separately neither of them fully explains the phenomena of light, but together they do."[48]

To draw a parallel between these two seemingly unrelated subjects of light and consciousness building, let's think of

---

[48]Einstein, Albert and Leopold Infeld. 1967. *The Evolution of Physics*. Touchstone

intellectual information as particle-based, i.e., words with specific meanings formed into ideas communicated to others. The ideas contained in books are examples of particle-based information. In contrast, let's think of intuitive learning as wave-based, subjective enlightenment that cannot be transmitted like a particle from one person to another. The particle-based information in this book may inspire you to turn within and open your intuitive portal to a genuine spiritual experience, but it cannot give you that experience.

Those who fail to open their intuitive portal by taking the intellectual approach to a spiritual experience will likely conclude that adding more particle-based information will produce the desired wave experience. Since the experience of the wave seems so elusive, the logical conclusion is that more time and the accumulation of more particles will solve the problem. Those who open their intuitive faculty to an experience of their soul, on the other hand, understand what the writer of Proverbs had in mind when he wrote:

> "Drink water from your own cistern, flowing water from your own well."[49]

What is needed is not more time and study, but greater intuitive sensitivity. So now we are left with a dilemma similar to Einstein's:

> Two contradictory pictures of the human being which, considered separately, neither fully explains us, but together they do.

We have an intuitive side and we have an intellectual side. How do we reconcile the two? We do this by seeing the soul as a wave expressing through a world that thinks and communicates in the language of the particle-based intellect. Separately neither of these aspects fully explains the human condition, but together they do. The wave (soul), takes on a particle-based interface (consciousness) to express itself, and to interact with a particle-centered culture and environment. In other words, sometimes we behave like a wave and sometimes we behave like a particle.

The soul-based, intuitive method of consciousness building

---

[49] Proverbs 5:15

draws ideas from the *ocean* of God via the soul. This is inspiration, intuitive knowing. Communicating wave-based knowledge requires a particle-based understanding of how to use language to express abstract ideas to a particle-oriented audience. This is why Jesus relied on the particle imagery of the parable intended to convey some facet of a wave-based reality. As inspired ideas rise from the soul and integrate into our consciousness, our understanding of the particle-based culture enhances our soul's ability to communicate and interface with the world.

Jesus expressed well this intuitive, inner oriented way of knowing:

> "It is written in the prophets, 'And they shall all be taught by God.' Every one who has heard and learned from the Father comes to me."[50]

Being taught by God is consciousness building through drawing ideas intuitively from the soul. Those who have already done this, those who have *"heard and learned from the Father,"* will recognize and respond to the kind of instruction Jesus described.

In the fourth chapter of John, Jesus used the particle-based imagery of water to illustrate these two ways of learning:

> "Every one who drinks of this water [from the public well, the intellectually driven culture] will thirst again, but whoever drinks of the water that I shall give him [soul-based, intuitive learning] will never thirst; the water that I shall give him will become in him a spring of water welling up to eternal life."[51]

Disconnected from all but a vague awareness of the soul, we interpret this thirst as the need to strengthen and improve the self-image. The self-image believes the more it accomplishes in the world, the more prosperous, attractive, successful, and less thirsty it will become.

Our longing to have and be more is the soul's natural action of nudging our awareness. Becoming sensitive to this nudging is the most effective, highest approach to spiritual understanding. The water Jesus gave us is the teaching that encourages us to

---

[50] John 6:45
[51] John 4:13-14

acknowledge and recognize the source of this nudging, that our desire to be more is the radiance of the soul, the inner "kingdom" that James described as:

> "... the perfect gift... from above, coming down from the Father of lights with whom there is no variation or shadow due to change."[52]

Though eclipsed by the clamoring distractions of the self-image, the soul is perpetual, eternal, an inner spring that rises into our awareness as a very different alternative to life as we generally think of it. The world's wells do not contain the thirst-quenching waters the soul provides. Regardless of how far we stray from this renewing spring, its waters still bubble forth. We will learn to listen and commit to understand the source of this internal thirst; we will come to know that the very thing we have been seeking in life is the soul that has been guiding us all along.

Because we have placed our soul on an evolutionary timeline, we return often, and in vain, to the public well of the senses. We have lost sight of the truth that our thirst for being and having more is simply the soul asserting itself. How and why this has happened is the topic we will explore in the next chapter.

---

[52] James 1:17

CHAPTER 5

THE MYTH OF SOUL EVOLUTION

The concept of soul evolution is derived from the belief that the average individual is presently spiritually incomplete but moving toward a state of illumination or completeness. We measure our perceived incompleteness against some ideal—a larger-than-life view of Jesus—contrasting the spiritual accomplishments portrayed in the Gospels with the rest of us who, by some accounts, have fallen into the grip of sin and death. The spiritual secularist, taking a different view, sees the intellectually advanced human race ready to blossom into a more spiritually illumined state. Whatever its origins, we consider spiritual growth as the process of becoming more like some advanced ideal.

Soul evolution creates the need for a contrived time line that is more suited to our biological rather than the spiritual level. Science associates the beginning of life with the rudimentary, bacterial forms, *stromatolites*, similar to those still found in such places as Hamelin Pool, in Shark Bay, on Australia's western coast. In contrast, spiritual discernment reveals that the life, love, power and intelligence that is the Creative Life Force we call God is a self-existent, self-sustaining *causal* energy that generates all physical form. This, I believe, is what the writer of Genesis was saying with his, "*In the beginning, God ...*" opening.

I am not, like science, implying that the human soul evolved from lower to higher biological forms. What I am suggesting is that understanding the soul as an individualized expression of this underlying Reality means that our soul has existed in its fullness prior to the advent of the human race as we know it. The soul has always existed, but began incarnating on this planet only when the environment reached a point where it was able to sustain the human organism. We know there are many forms of life that can thrive in environments toxic to the human being. Early earth was without oxygen and lay exposed to the full brunt of the sun's radiation. The soul would have no incentive to take up a body in such a biologically hostile environment.

Since the dawn of recorded history, people have been reporting mystical experiences, levels of awareness and intuitive ways of knowing that transcend the usual intellectual methods of learning. The consistency in the language of mystics indicates that the elements that make up this deeper awareness have been present for at least as long as we humans have been recording our experience, and probably much longer. If we examine scripture and first-person accounts from the beginning of history to the present, we find that nothing about the mystical experience has changed. The Hindu *Vedas*, for example, dating from 1700-1100 BCE, hold that the soul is inexhaustible and eternal. The *Bhagavad Gita*, believed to be composed at a much later date, expresses the same idea, that the soul transcends the body into which it incarnates:

> "For the atman [soul, self] there is neither birth nor death at any time. He has not come into being, does not come into being, and will not come into being. He is unborn, eternal, ever – existing and primeval. He is not slain when the body is slain."[53]

Jesus seemed to be making the presumption of the soul's preexistence when he said to the Jews, *"Truly, truly, I say to you, before Abraham was, I am."*[54] If we can accept that our soul predates our current body, is it not conceivable that it predates all other living forms and all bodies that we may have inhabited?

The particle-based language and the metaphors used to describe the spiritual experience have changed somewhat with the times, but the wave-based experience that we attempt to describe through the

---

[53] Bhagavad Gita. Chapter 2, Verse 20
[54] John 8:58

language has not. The faculties of mind needed to experience the soul have always been in place and are fully in place now.

It is easy to see why we have placed the soul on an evolutionary track. Biological evolution, supported by countless facts, makes it impossible to deny. Through a careful examination of the fossil record, we can reconstruct a plausible explanation of the dawn of the human race. Following the trail of artifacts, anthropologists know about when our ancestors began using fire, making tools, utilizing agriculture, creating art, and burying their dead—acts we associate with the evolution of human intelligence. In today's modern spiritual commercialism, evolution is a major selling buzzword. Slick websites and magazines entice readers to become part of the affluent, *advancing* global consciousness that promises to *activate our soul's purpose,* and *manifest our creative destiny.* It seems logical to place the soul on the same evolutionary track.

I would argue that focus on the evolving brain and intellect has diverted our attention away from our fully developed spiritual capacity and drawn our focus to the ever-changing, intellectually gleaned information that dominates our interest. I am not implying, of course, that the evolution of the intellect is a spiritual impairment. I am saying that the spiritual faculty is not a new sense that, like tool making, art, or technology, is only now emerging through an advancing human consciousness. This deluge of senses-based information has simply eclipsed the intuitive faculty native to our being.

Emilie Cady warned her readers that they would not glean spiritual understanding from the intellectual pursuit:

> What is this understanding on the getting of which depends so much? Is it intellectual lore, obtained from delving deep into books of other men's, rocks (geology), or stars (astronomy), or even the human body (physiology)? Nay, verily, for when did such knowledge ever insure life and health and peace, ways of pleasantness, with riches and honor?[55]

What some are seeing as a newly evolving spiritual faculty is but an intellectually contrived replica, a *pseudo-soul,* routinely mistaken for the genuine article. The spiritual dimension, though masked by

---

[55] Lessons in Truth. Unity Books

a contrived façade of religious beliefs and senses-based perceptions deemed spiritual wisdom, has always been active at some level of human consciousness.

The book of Judges concludes with, *"In those days there was no king in Israel; everyone did what was right in his own eyes."*[56] In other words, this author was lamenting the lack of a spiritual anchor among his people. Perhaps they were directed by something akin to the prevailing logic of the sixties: *If it feels good, do it.* The intellect not anchored in the soul is destined to follow the ever-changing, contrived replica, the idol in any of its myriad forms, far removed from the true governance of the actual soul. This is what we see in much of today's New Age smorgasbord.

The rational mind, disconnected from its intuitive counterpart, treats the subject of spirituality as a peripheral, with the intellect as the center. The intellect thrives on books and practices touting spirituality, but is itself incapable of wading into an experiential unity with the light it craves. This is the appeal of the seminar, the gathering, where people surround themselves with like-minded seekers, experience an emotional high, and leave believing they have made some level of spiritual progress.

To understand our solar system, we start at its gravitational center, the sun. Remove a few planets and the sun remains unaffected. Take away the sun and all the planets fly into oblivion. In earlier periods, people believed the earth, not the sun, was the center of the solar system. This reasoning made the sun a peripheral rather than the central, life-sustaining engine of our planetary system. As logical as it seemed at the time, we know today this earth-centered paradigm was erroneous.

The same holds true in our spiritual reasoning. When we attempt to make the intellect the starting point of our spiritual understanding, we are trying to make the peripheral central, trying to turn a light-reflecting planet into a life-giving sun. The self-image considers the intellectual endeavor the supreme way of knowing, impeding our attempts to establish a consciousness grounded in the soul.

The field of neuroscience continues to produce an impressive and interesting array of intriguing facts about the marvelous workings of the brain. This type of knowledge is fascinating, but

---

[56] Judges 21:25

the growing field of near-death research is moving beyond the brain as causal, and focusing on that which continues to function as consciousness when the brain literally shuts down. It is from this basis—consciousness existing independent of the brain—that we must begin our quest to understand the human being.

The Fall

Spiritual traditions that see God as separate from the individual, and this will include most, hold that some sort of time-space barrier stands between the individual and the ultimate solution to their problem. Something must happen now, or in the near future, that will allow us to rise above the current problem of separation and experience relief from our suffering. The thing that must happen becomes our plan of salvation, the means through barriers of sin or spiritual ignorance that stand between our ultimate good and ourselves.

The Judeao-Christian tradition traces the origin of separation from God to Adam and Eve's disobedience by eating the fruit of the tree of knowledge of good and evil, an action they were plainly warned to not take. Whether we take this story literally or metaphorically, the sources of the many hardships we associate with the human condition today began with disobedience to God.

> "… cursed is the ground because of you; in toil you shall eat of it all the days of your life; thorns and thistles it shall bring forth to you; and you shall eat the plants of the field. In the sweat of your face you shall eat bread till you return to the ground, for out of it you were taken; you are dust, and to dust you shall return."[57]

The ancient Hebrew offered this allegory as their explanation of why life in the body is often difficult. The answer is that humankind, from the very beginning, disobeyed God. From the Jewish perspective, the plan of resolution to this problem involves a concerted effort to live according to God's law as given through the scriptures. Traditional Christianity's answer to returning to God is the acceptance of Jesus' death on the cross as a sacrifice for one's sins. For those who take the more metaphysical approach to

---

[57] Gen. 3:17-19

Christian dogma, the story becomes an allegorical depiction of our fall away from the awareness of God as our source. We implement the plan of resolution through meditation, spiritual studies, and the schooling provided through life's many lessons.

The influence of this serpent, variously designated as carnal mind, the sinful nature, and race consciousness is the belief that the quality of one's life improves *primarily* through some sort of material acquisition. The serpent promises great results from eating this material fruit. Rather than learn from our universal mother's succumbing to temptation, we unfortunate humans get constant reminders from our religious leaders that we inherited Eve's weakness and the willful compliance of her husband. None, since our ill-fated couple, has been without the need of salvation from whatever version of separation we embrace.

We can see in this story a metaphorical parallel to the birth of the self-image. Eve sees three reasons why the fruit of the tree of knowledge of good and evil is good to eat:

> "So when the woman saw that the tree was (1) good for food, and that it was (2) a delight to the eyes, and that (3) the tree was to be desired to make one wise, she took of its fruit and ate; and she also gave some to her husband, and he ate."[58]

The fruit is nutritious, will make one wise, and it is a delight to the eye. In other words, accomplishments and the acquisition of external things appear to be satisfying, enlightening, and attractive enough to give a boost to our self-image.

When Adam and Eve ate the fruit,

> "... the eyes of both were opened, and they knew that they were naked; and they sewed fig leaves together and made themselves aprons."[59]

This sudden awareness of the condition of nakedness represents the consequence of the identity down-shifting from the soul to the self-image. Adam and Eve immediately experienced lack, a condition hitherto unknown. This shift is accompanied by the self-image's standard of values that measures self-worth on the

---

[58] Genesis 3:6
[59] Gen. 3:7

dualistic scale of *have* and *have not* (knowing good and evil). They attempt to compensate for this feeling of inadequacy (nakedness) by clothing themselves in fig leaves (material acquisitions, positions of power and intellectual knowledge).

The cherubim and the flaming sword that turns every way, bar Adam and Eve from the tree of life.[60] Though this sounds like punishment, it only points to the simple fact that the senses-based self-image cannot partake of the fruit of the tree of life and then live forever. The soul and the senses-based self-image are incompatible. They can never evolve into a state of unity.

Self-Awareness

In the opening chapter I wrote, *"In my own way, I was moving my self-awareness from a pail-centered self-image to its true ocean-water foundation, the soul."* It is our self-awareness, the *I*, that eventually lets go of the self-image and returns to its rightful alliance with the soul. We do this through the practice of meditation (Chapters 10 & 11), which is less a process of learning new information, and more a recovery endeavor.

Self-awareness is the capacity for introspection, the observation or examination of one's own mental and emotional states and processes. Self-awareness also creates the sense of oneself as an individual. The problem is that our self-awareness focuses on our sensory experiences. The senses report that we are not merely separate from our environment and other individuals, but that we are also separate from the spiritual reality to which we owe our existence. The narrow gate of the intuition closes and the wide gate of the senses-driven intellect and emotion rules, elevating material appearances to the rational mind's working model of reality. The soul itself, judging reality by a different standard, is relegated to an inconsequential abstraction. The senses-derived self-image becomes the ruling force, its development and bolstering, our primary focus.

We struggle with the meditative process because we attempt to access the tree of life, the soul, from the subconscious storehouse of intellectually gleaned concepts rather than through the intuitive portal that leads to the soul's inner sanctum. We are confronted by the cherubim and the flaming sword which turns every way, that

---

[60] Gen. 3:24

busy mind that throws out a plethora of distractions that block access. The truth is that Paul's "*unspiritual man*" never fell from the Garden because he was never there in the first place. The garden to which he hopes to return is a phantom, a daydream conjured up by the mistaken hope that the self-image will one day attain the status of the soul, a false hope that has given rise to the metaphysical community's nearly universal acceptance of soul evolution. We have been convinced that if this unspiritual man studies enough and fills itself with enough spiritually accurate information, it will "*receive the gifts of the Spirit of God.*" The false hope of the self-image is to one day become what the soul already is.

The spiritual journey is not about reaching some kind of critical mass that tips the scale by filling the self-image with spiritually accurate information. It's about moving the awareness to its rightful foundation of the spiritually sound soul. The self-image and all its many aspirations are to be completely let go.

The *fall* is a depiction of the central *I* migrating from the all-sustaining soul to the senses-based self-image where its sustenance is gleaned from external sources. This migration begins in childhood and continues throughout the so-called formative years. The soul struggles to acclimate to having taken on a physical body subject to scientific, medical, and educational fields firmly grounded in senses-based materialism.

The value of this aspect of the materialistic approach is undeniable. It is also worth noting that before the world moved to this material model, our philosophical roots were firmly grounded in the understanding of the spiritual and material realms as independent domains. In philosophy, *panpsychism*—the view that consciousness was the universal feature of all things—was the default theory. The spiritual rather than the material realm was the accepted source of all that is seen, the foundation upon which the visible world rested.

This shift favoring materialism occurred largely because a substantial sector of our brain-based material science has taught for generations that our belief in the spiritual realm is, as one writer puts it, little more than "*the product of an evolutionary adaptation, a coping mechanism that emerged to help humankind deal with the fear of death.*"[61] From this reductionist point of view, consciousness, like life itself,

---

[61] Alper, Matthew. 2008. *The God Part of the Brain.* Sourcebooks

arises from a physical basis. We owe our very existence to our brain. That this assumption is strictly theoretical is irrelevant to those in the scientific community who deal with the problem of consciousness by either explaining it away as a byproduct of brain-function, or by ignoring it altogether.

Despite this disinterest, a growing number of voices in science recognize that we cannot understand consciousness merely from a physical basis. David Chalmers, philosopher and cognitive scientist, has designated consciousness *the hard problem* we cannot simply pass over. Robert Lanza, deemed one of the most respected scientists in the world, and co-author Robert Berman, considered the world's most widely read astronomer, agree. In their book, *Biocentrism: How Life and Consciousness are the Keys to Understanding the True Nature of the Universe*,[62] they lay out an excellent case in support of the notion that consciousness, not matter, provides the underpinning of our universe. They ask, *"Has anyone explained how dumb carbon, hydrogen, and oxygen molecules could have, by combining accidentally, become sentient—aware!—and then utilized this sentience to acquire a taste for hot dogs and the blues?"*

Near-death and Brain Research

The scientific approach to near-death research challenges orthodox presumptions of both the scientist and the spiritual evolutionist. From the scientific viewpoint, consciousness cannot exist without a brain. Near-death research, on the other hand, is providing evidence that consciousness can exist apart from the brain. One of the most famous cases, reported by many near-death researchers, is that of Pam Reynolds.

> Reynolds reported to her physician that she was experiencing symptoms of dizziness, loss of speech and difficulty in moving parts of her body. Her physician referred her to a neurologist and a CAT scan later revealed that Reynolds had a large aneurysm in her brain, close to the brain stem. Because of the difficult position of the aneurysm, Reynolds was predicted to have no chance of survival. As a last resort, Robert F. Spetzler — a neurosurgeon of the Barrow Neurological Institute in Phoenix, Arizona — decided that a

---

[62] Lanza, Robert, Robert Berman. 2010. *Biocentrism: How Life and Consciousness are the Keys to Understanding the True Nature of the Universe.* BenBella Books

rarely performed surgical procedure, known as hypothermic cardiac arrest, was necessary to improve Pam's outcome. During this procedure, also known as a standstill operation, Pam's body temperature was lowered to 50 °F (10 °C), her breathing and heartbeat stopped, and the blood drained from her head. Her eyes were closed with tape and small ear plugs with speakers were placed in her ears. These speakers emitted audible clicks which were used to check the function of the brain stem to ensure that she had a flat EEG — or a non-responsive brain — before the operation proceeded. The operation was a success and Reynolds recovered completely. The total surgery lasted about 7 hours with a few complications along the way.

Reynolds reported that during the operation she heard a sound like a natural 'D' that seemed to pull her out of her body and allowed her to "float" above the operating room and watch the doctors perform the operation. Reynolds claims that during this time she felt "more aware than normal" and her vision was more focused and clearer than normal vision. Reynolds says she was able to identify surgical instruments and hear conversations between operating room staff.[63]

The spiritual evolutionist holds that a future state, gradually attainable by the soul, will be far superior to the state thus far achieved. Again, near-death research challenges this assumption by exposing the fact that the soul is already functioning at a level that defies current models of both brain science and the spiritual evolutionist. From my study of this research, I have concluded that the soul not only has the capacity to exist apart from the brain, but the evidence strongly suggests that the brain and its physical senses actually hinder the full functionality of consciousness.

Further, our belief that the soul has lessons to learn from the material plane has done nothing to improve, harm, or reduce the already advanced condition of the soul. Near-death experiencers routinely report the feeling of having come home, of experiencing a reality far more substantial than the physical environment, of being more alive than ever, and of having a level of sensory

---

[63] Wikipedia: Pam Reynolds Case. For a full account of this fascinating case, see page 171 of *Consciousness Beyond Life,* by Dr. Pim Van Lommel. HarperOne.

perception (360 degree vision, for example) that defies our current understanding. Conditions of physical atrophy—use it or lose it— apparently do not apply at the soul level.

We can link the quality of our material environment to the positive or negative influence of our belief system, but we cannot do the same with the soul. Our soul remains unaffected by false beliefs, negative thinking, and any material restrictions these may have imposed. Attempting to force correlations between the condition of the soul, our shortsighted belief system, and material conditions is the primary mistake made by those teachers of spiritual principles who apply senses-based logic to their mythology of soul development. It seems, *"the mystery hidden for ages and generations"* that was grasped by the likes of Paul, has once again slipped from our mainstream thinking. *"Christ in you, the hope of glory"* now dangles from a pole at the end of a very long evolutionary journey, the end of which is not possible to reach.

In the following chapter, we will explore the main points of soul evolution and consider how our body-based cultural influence contributed to our adopting them. We will then examine some freeing alternatives that are more in alignment with the truth of the complete soul.

CHAPTER 6

EXPLORING THE MYTH

Prevailing New Thought logic assumes that, because like attracts like, our physicality is the result of our soul vibrating at a slower, materialistic, thus inferior level. According to this model, until the soul sufficiently evolves, the negative cycles of birth, death, and rebirth continue. Charles Fillmore, realizing at the end of his life he had not achieved the level of soul regeneration that would eternally perpetuate his body, said he would be back, next time with "... *a perfect body.*" This statement, as we have seen, contradicts the teaching he passed on to others. By his own standard, he could not return with a perfect body, for "*awakening cannot be associated with dying.*" He would "*come forth ... unto the resurrection of damnation...*" for, as he taught, "*everyone begins where he left off.*"

If soul evolution were indeed a fact, then it is not, as many spiritual teachers advocate, a human problem. It is the problem of whatever force is driving the evolutionary phenomenon. How could a single personality thwart the forward movement of a cosmic process we did not put in motion? Are we to assume there is some external entity pushing us into physical expression with the hope that if we succeed *it* will succeed, and if we fail *it* will fail? I don't think so. As I think about the mind-boggling epochs of geological time, and how countless species have come into being, been wiped out, and then risen again in different forms, the negative thinking of a single individual seems but a trite blip that has little if any relevance in the grander scheme.

If you stand next to a river, do you think that even with your clearest visualization and the affirmative power of your spoken word, you could block or even slow down the water's flow? The power that moves the water is unaffected by any action of your mind. Your soul is much more powerful and persistent than the mightiest of rivers.

The belief that we can encourage or hinder any perceived process of soul evolution is a declaration of the existence of *two* powers rather than our usual *one Presence and one Power.* One power initiates the evolutionary process and another (in this case, our thinking) can prevent or at least hinder it through life's lessons missed, ignored, and otherwise unlearned. Does this not boil down to human will having the power to trump the will of God?

There is another, much simpler way to approach this problem. It is not our soul, but our *perception* of the soul that is affected by our thinking. We do not stop the river; we only give ourselves the false impression that we in some way affect it.

If the soul is complete, then why don't we experience it? The spiritual evolutionist attributes the feeling of soul incompleteness to spiritual immaturity, a problem resolved through further learning. Some learning is obviously required, but before we declare ourselves incomplete, we need to consider what actually happens when we learn something.

Discovering the true nature of an object does not change the object. It changes the way we understand the object. When we learned that the earth was round rather than flat, nothing about the earth itself changed. Our thinking that it was flat did not make it flat. Nor did our realization that the earth was round suddenly make it round. The revelation of our round earth changed only the way we related to it. We no longer feared sending ships over that imagined abyss of the horizon.

Likewise, our thinking the soul is either evolving or already complete does not alter the condition of the soul. Our thinking only impacts how we view and approach the problem. The soul itself is complete regardless of what we think.

Why does this matter? Our view of the soul's condition affects the way we approach everything from meditation, to spiritual healing, to prosperity, to considering our soul's purpose for showing up on this planet in the first place. If we think of the soul as *"the light* [that] *shines in the darkness and the darkness has not overcome it,"*[64] we position our mind in a receptive mode that receives the truth of this light. We do not seek to make it true or even feel compelled to learn why it is true. As Cady writes, *"You will know* [the truth of this light] *just as you know that you are alive. All the argument in the world to convince you against Truth that comes to you through direct revelation will fall flat and harmless at your side."*[65]

If we are praying for guidance, for example, we let the truth of the soul's completeness impress our intuitive faculty with the soul's spiritual counterpart to the thing or condition we seek. This aspect of our request is ours already. The inner fulfillment we experience in quiet receptivity translates into the mental, emotional, and material equivalent that enables us to see our way. There are times, as Cady suggests, when we take no action, when the Spirit moving through us does the work, and there are other times when we are inspired to act. In truth, we have never been without guidance. Our lack of clarity is the result of our searching through our surface experience for something that has always existed in our depths.

As in our earth analogy, our revolution in knowledge that the earth was round was simply the act of bringing our thinking into alignment with that which had been true from the beginning. This change of thought did not change the shape or location of the earth, but it profoundly changed the way we related to it. Likewise, we can neither hinder nor accelerate the perceived process of soul growth because the soul, like the round earth, is already all that it ever needs to be.

The Ugly Duckling Revisited

In my first book on meditation and prayer, I referred to Hans Christian Andersen's tale of the ugly duckling. The little swan's life did not work well as long as he attempted to fit into the duck culture *as a duck.* He did not become successful until he stumbled onto the wisdom expressed in the ancient Greek axiom, *Know Thyself.* When the swan realized the truth of what he was, earth-life became something much different. His life started working.

Do we not often try to make sense of the world thinking like ducks (evolving souls) when we are really swans (complete souls)?

---

[64] John 1:5
[65] Lessons In Truth

We find ourselves living reactionary lives, looking at all events as if they can teach us how to better conform to the duck culture (senses-based standards), all the while dreaming of becoming swans. Embracing the understanding that we are now swans who have incarnated simply because we wanted to have this earthly experience enables us to stop constantly trying to force from our circumstances things that will make our lives as ducks more fulfilling. We begin asking what we, as swans, want to do with the life we are now living.

Our soul did not come to conform to either environmental or cultural conditions. Though specific environmental conditions are required to accommodate the body, they are not required to accommodate the soul. The soul, in all its wisdom, exists with or without a body and the earth that supports it. The greatest gift we bring to our world is that of divesting ourselves of the need to be something we are not, and dare to live out of our true swan identity. We do the world no service by gaining the approval as a duck while losing our identity as a swan.

Earth Influence

It should come as no surprise that our experience on this earth has prompted a perception of reality heavily influenced by both our body and our environment. Certain things appear to be true of the soul because we view them from a body perspective. Age, skin color, gender, body height and weight, hair and eye color, as we have seen, heavily influence the self-image. We declare a person born when their body emerges from the womb, dead when their soul vacates the body, and we celebrate everything in between as the sum of who they were. It is difficult to think of any aspect of our life without considering the various influences of the body.

Think about your spiritual quest and the body-related issues you hope to resolve. Our prayers for healing, prosperity, and harmony in relationships nearly always feature the body as the central focus. The spiritual ends we pursue are often responses to the body's needs.

This influence extends into our environment as well. We take for granted the reality of day and night because we experience the world from the perspective of a body bound to a spinning planet. If we could rise high enough above earth's influence, we would only experience perpetual sunlight. The twenty-four hour day and its offspring of weeks, months, and years would disappear.

Another indicator of the body's tremendous influence arises as the most common complaint concerning meditation. We can't stop thinking about our body-centered life. If we consider the amount of time daily we spend thinking about feeding, clothing, sheltering, and transporting the body, it makes these words of Jesus sound like wishful thinking:

> "Therefore I tell you, do not be anxious about your life, what you shall eat or what you shall drink, nor about your body, what you shall put on. Is not life more than food, and the body more than clothing?"[66]

Having stepped into this moth and rust-laden mechanical domain of Newtonian physics and into a body that demands such an extraordinary amount of care and attention, is it any wonder that we have dropped the soul into this evolutionary mix more appropriately applied to the body?

The Fact of Physical Evolution

The study of evolution provides a fascinating perspective of our geological and biological past. Unlike the strict advocates of biblical creationism, I have no trouble believing the earth has been roughly 4.6 billion years in the making, or that life forms began simply, possibly in volcanically charged hot springs, or in ocean depths beyond the reach of light. It boggles the mind to think that dinosaurs inhabited this planet for a hundred-million years. To consider how living organisms first developed, survived numerous mass extinctions, made spectacular comebacks as completely different plant and animal types, and then went on to achieve the astounding level of diversity we see today is, for me, a source of endless wonder.

Despite my tremendous respect for all of its many disciplines, I think it is shortsighted of science to routinely mark the beginning of life as that moment, some 3.6 billion years ago, when the first simple celled creatures appeared. I realize that science is obligated by its own materialistic rules to treat life as a byproduct of organic processes rather than as causal in nature. That bits of matter

---

[66] Matthew 6:25

somehow contained the intelligence to assemble even the simplest life forms is a presumption that science has neither adequately explained nor duplicated in the laboratory. For all their elaborate theories, and there are many, the explanation (usually accompanied with a shrug) is, *somehow it just happened.*

The fire of life did indeed unite with the tinder of matter and flamed up into the diversity of living forms we see today. It is refreshing to see representatives of the hard sciences step forward with alternative explanations. Again, referencing the work of biologist Robert Lanza and astronomer Bob Berman, these authors point to the work of physicist John Wheeler in support of their belief that *"life is not an accidental byproduct of physics"* that *"life and consciousness are absolutely fundamental to our understanding of the universe."*

> "Going even further, the late physicist John Wheeler (1911-2008), who coined the term "black hole," advocated what is now called the Participatory Anthropic Principle (PAP): observers are required to bring the universe into existence. Wheeler's theory says that any pre-life Earth would have existed in an indeterminate state .... Once an observer exists, the aspects of the universe under observation become forced to resolve into one state, a state that includes a seemingly pre-life Earth."[67]

Are we witnessing science coming full circle to one of philosophy's oldest notions: that consciousness, distinct from matter, is a stand-alone, fundamental element permeating all aspects of our universe? The ability to observe one's corpse from a corner in the ceiling, after all, obviously points to the fact that there are aspects of consciousness still begging explanation. What Thales, Plato, Spinoza, Leibniz, or William James might have taken in stride, the material scientist has until now been prone to dismiss.

Adapting to the Present Environment

I believe it is our affinity and respect for the evidence-based methodology of science that has prompted the metaphysical community to mingle the ideas of biological and soul evolution

---

[67] Berman, Bob; Lanza, Robert (2010-02-02). Biocentrism: How Life and Consciousness are the Keys to Understanding the True Nature of the Universe (p. 90). BenBella Books, Inc.. Kindle Edition.

into a logical marriage. Plato, in his *theory of forms*, taught that ideas were pure mental forms of the highest kind of reality, and that certain kinds of preexisting ideas imprinted on the soul prior to its physical incarnation. Charles Fillmore seemed to echo this when he wrote, "*Divine mind has placed in the mind of everyone an image of the perfect-man body.*"[68] In whatever way this mind/body connection originated, it is clear that Fillmore thought of the body as an inextricable extension of the soul. Taking this idea to another level, we have seen that he added his belief that the onset of aging and death represented a soul that did not yet have a firm grasp on the principle of life, an absolute requirement for expressing the perfect body idea.

The material scientist, on the other hand, under no obligation to make the body/soul connection, acknowledges that a primary driving force of biological evolution has nothing to do with a soul-implanted blueprint attempting to work itself out. The driving force is *adaptation* to the dynamics of a given environment, a process biologists refer to as *phenotypic plasticity*. All organisms, including ours, take their cues of form and functional adaptation from their present environment.

This is why the architecture of a home on the Florida coast, for example, is not the same as a home in the mountains. A single individual can own both homes and choose their own décor. The actual design of each home, however, is environmentally driven.

The hard-core metaphysician will dismiss this fact outright, insisting that adaptation is an inside out, unfolding process. It is probably more accurate to say that the forces that shape our bodies are not spiritually but environmentally driven. The body, not the soul, must be compatible with its environment.

It is true that our state of mind affects the body. Who hasn't experienced the occasional headache, the tightened stomach, or the physical lethargy brought on by depression? We can literally worry ourselves into a heart attack. The mistake we make here is that we equate our state of mind with the state of our soul. Regardless of our state of mind, positive or negative, the state of our soul remains unaffected. We are dealing with two parallel but very different spheres: spirit and matter, soul and body. Because each sphere is governed by its own set of laws, it makes perfect sense to

---

[68] Atom Smashing Power of Mind

"Render therefore to Caesar the things that are Caesar's [the realm of matter], *and to God the things that are God's"* [the realm of spirit].[69]

The Body Will Never Express the Capacity of the Soul

The spiritual evolutionist presumes the soul will one day be so highly evolved as to express the full spectrum of Christ consciousness through the body. This assumption, usually treated as a given, deserves to be challenged. The physical brain and body, regardless of how advanced they are, will never be able to express the infinite capacity of the soul. This is not what the physical organism is intended to do. Measuring the capacity or state of the soul by weighing it against the present capability and condition of the brain and body is like comparing the ocean to a puddle of water.

In one sense, we pay the price of restriction for taking on a body, but what we gain is the ability to experience this plane in a way we could not otherwise. The body will never reach the point where it can fully accommodate the soul's capacity, a fact we should not mistake as evidence of an unevolved soul.

If you decide to go on a sightseeing tour, you jump in your car and take off. When your interest in travel begins to wane, you stop. No one considers it negative that you drive a car because you cannot yet mentally transport your body from one location to another. Why should we think of the body any differently?

Philosophers have long accepted that each person has a spiritual or astral body not subject to material laws and the normal restrictions of time, space, and gravity (not to mention illness, fatigue, hunger, etc). Trying to make the physical body perform like the spiritual body is redundant and totally misses the purpose of the physical body. For all its imagined capabilities—and I believe these are extraordinary—there is one thing the spiritual body cannot do that the physical body can. *The spiritual body cannot interface with the material plane.* The physical body has but one purpose and that purpose is to allow interaction with the material realm. When we reach a point where we would rather levitate than walk, we will stop incarnating.

---

[69] Matthew 22:21

The Body is a Choice

I want to close this chapter by sharing a few thoughts on the idea that we incarnated by choice, that we did so with the full understanding of the limitations and drawbacks involved. By this, I do not mean we knew we would have abusive parents, for example, or that we would suffer some handicap, or that we chose these or other issues for the lessons our soul needed. I realize some people draw comfort, even closure from this idea. Like many in my profession, I once embraced this theory as a way of helping others make sense of difficult experiences. Now I see this as an unnecessary spinoff of the evolutionary model. The idea of the complete soul offers a more spiritually productive, logical, and fulfilling perspective. From this starting point, logic dictates that further incarnations, with whatever experiences they hold, will not make the soul more complete. A full pail, after all, can hold no more water.

Someone will ask, if our soul did not come for the lessons life has to offer, then why would we go to the trouble of incarnating? I've given this question a lot of thought over the years, and I believe the answer is a lot less complicated than the evolving soul model allows. For reasons of our choosing, we came simply because we wanted to be here. Getting here meant we needed a vehicle, a way to bring our soul from the spiritual to the material plane. The most efficient way of doing this is through a body.

Saying the body is the most efficient way of bringing the soul into expression doesn't mean that our experience of incarnating has been perfect. Stepping into the body vehicle made us susceptible to rough roads and all kinds of foul weather, so much so that the bulk of our attention has gone to the maintenance needs of the body vehicle and its journey, while the soul, in a sense, remains nearly unnoticed in the cargo hold.

A major pitfall of the evolving soul model is that it makes the spiritual experience about the vehicle, its journey, and the belief that we will one day arrive at some special destination on this earthly sojourn. The truth is we have arrived. We've been so busy looking for specific conditions on this planet that we have forgotten that earth itself is our destination. We didn't come to experience life from the cab of this delivery truck, driving endlessly from one place to another, looking for the right location to offload and unpack our cargo. We came here to experience life *from* our soul, right here and right now, using this body vehicle as our means of being here.

I said earlier that we are here for reasons of our choosing. We may doubt this because, unlike picking last year's vacation spot, we have no clear memory of making such a decision. This memory is there, however, embedded in those things that truly interest and come most natural to us. These things do not boost our egos, advance our positions, or make us feel powerful. These are the things we quietly and reverently give our time and attention to without pay, persuasion, or recognition.

I see in the process of writing books some useful parallels that may help shed light on our reasons for incarnating. People write books for all kinds of reasons. Some write for sheer entertainment, others for educational purposes. Still others combine education with entertainment. I write because I want to share ideas that I think are important and will be of value to my readers. Sharing these ideas requires a way of doing that and the book is my vehicle of choice. Writing a book is fraught with challenges. It involves embodying inspired ideas in words, sentences, paragraphs, and chapters that create a cohesive presentation one can read on a bus.

In the beginning of this section, I said we incarnated by choice, and that we did so with the full understanding of the limitations and drawbacks involved. I say this in the context similar to that of writing a book. When I made the decision to undertake this project, I knew from previous experience the nature of the challenges involved. Ideas often come in a flash and I can jot them down with relative ease. Including them in the context of a book is another matter. This can take hours, days, weeks, even months to accomplish. I have spent days working on a single paragraph only to delete it later. What comes quite easy on one level, is not so easy to express on another.

If we think of the soul as a set of ideas and the body as the book (our means of literally publishing the soul to the world), then we see the challenges we encounter in this incarnating/publishing process have little if anything to do with the soul itself. The ideas I want to convey through a book are largely unaffected by my struggle to convey them.

It is our associations of soul with body (our body-based self-image) that make our body-oriented challenges feel so personal. We mistakenly associate these challenges with the condition of our soul, but a clear understanding of the difference spares us this unneeded stress. Having great ideas is not the same as having the ability to put them in writing. This is where the work comes in.

If, as I have suggested, you were unfortunate enough to have had the experience of abusive parents, you may have made the mistake of interpreting this situation as something your soul needed to learn from these people. Dysfunctional, abusive people have little or nothing to teach our soul. Assigning them the role of teacher is often an attempt to put a positive spin on destructive behavior we struggle to forgive, a willingness to blame ourselves so we can let them off the hook and move on. Genuine forgiveness, however, has nothing to do with making peace with the actions of another. Forgiveness occurs when we touch our own wholeness and realize that the power and soul integrity we thought they took from us has remained with us all along. They may indeed provide the catalyst that causes us to look deeper into our soul, but what we find is nothing they brought. Nor does their negative influence have the power to detract from our real purpose for incarnating. We did not need their negativity to enrich or advance our soul. If we are giving people and various conditions this kind of power, we ourselves are obscuring our purpose for incarnating. We're experiencing writer's block, so to speak, staring blankly out the window, hung up on some writing issue, while our book goes unpublished.

The specific issues we encountered by taking on a body were, in all likelihood, unknown to us. Our soul did not choose them for the growth opportunities they might offer. On the other hand, fully aware of our soul's completeness, we understood there would indeed be challenges associated with temporarily tethering this vast, nonlocalized essence we call our soul to a vehicle subject to the restrictive laws of time, space, and gravity. We are not here to work our way through the school of soul development, or to pay some karmic debt. We have incarnated for reasons similar to those I have agreed to take on when writing books: I do it because I want to. You and I are here because we made the choice to be here.

The importance of the framework of ideas through which we view our earthly experience and our reasons for taking it on cannot be overstated. In the next chapter, we will examine a Truth-based system that will shed light on the kinds of core values we hold and how they influence our experience.

CHAPTER 7

A PARADIGM SHIFT

Pilate said to him, "So you are a king?" Jesus answered, "You say that I am a king. For this I was born, and for this I have come into the world, to bear witness to the truth. Every one who is of the truth hears my voice." Pilate said to him, "What is truth?"[70]

When I refer to the complete soul, I'm saying that all your soul can ever be it is right now. In addition, all you will ever need to experience the full spectrum of your complete soul you now have. I understand that this runs counter to the experience of those who have but a vague understanding and virtually no illuminating experience of their soul. It challenges our intellectually grounded reasoning to state that spiritual wisdom is not found in our religious sanctuaries or within the ivory towers of academia. We experience the truth of our being by stilling the senses-based intellect and turning our awareness to that spiritual stratum where the natural wisdom of our fully functioning soul bubbles forth. It is here and here alone that we become *"of the truth"* that prompts us to sit up and take notice when the mystic speaks.

The above exchange between Jesus and Pilate reaches no

---

[70] John 18:37-38

conclusion as to what Jesus meant by the term *Truth*. Pilate may have been expressing sarcasm and he simply turned away assuming from his own experience in public office that the only truth that mattered was the kind that enhanced one's political popularity. Jesus may have remained silent knowing his answer would mean nothing to a man in Pilate's position. What we do glean from Jesus' statement is that he considered expressing his understanding of Truth to be the single most important aspect of his ministry, his very purpose in life. He also expressed the understanding that those whose spiritual eyes were open would resonate with his message.

This was my experience when I first read Emilie Cady's book, *Lessons in Truth*. I *heard* her voice. Despite the fact that her ideas found opposition from the spiritual authority in my life at the time, her message touched something in me that rang true. My minister, coming from his own understanding of Truth, assured me the book was the work of the devil. Though I was not yet equipped to explain why I knew he was wrong, I quietly departed that familiar path for one that would offer further exposure to Cady's way of thinking.

A frustration common to most in our early years of spiritual discovery is that we intuitively know more than we can explain. An idea we hear or read rings true, but we cannot say why. Our attempts to explain leave us babbling, sometimes argumentative. I once loaned Cady's book to a woman who promptly returned it, unread, with this complaint: *How can this woman be so arrogant? She thinks she's smart enough to give me lessons in Truth? Who does she think she is, God?*

Her questions and attitude surprised me, mainly because arrogance was never a quality I associated with Emilie Cady. I learned early that her interpretation of Truth was not for everyone. As I thought about this woman's reaction, I began to realize that Cady's personality wasn't the issue; it was the difference in our understanding of Truth, and in time, I would begin to see why this difference exists.

We run into difficulty defining Truth because we think of it as a single, all-encompassing reality that exists apart from *your* truth and *mine*, usually with the definition favoring *mine*. Many believe that if we could all somehow lay aside our preconceived notions and open our minds to this singular reality, we would come together on the common ground of Truth. The problem is, few seem to agree on what constitutes Truth.

Earlier I referenced physicist John Wheeler who advocated the belief that observers are required to bring the universe into existence (PAP: Participatory Anthropic Principle). As bizarre as this might sound, it may provide us with the kind of model that can help us understand what we mean when we use a word like Truth.

Truth, as we each understand it, is not a single idea, but the sum of a trinity of core values, a paradigm we use as the basis of logic we'll apply to all areas of our life. These core values consist of 1) our understanding of the nature of God, 2) our understanding of the nature of the individual, and 3) our understanding of the nature of the relationship between God and the individual.

In the context of spiritual considerations, there are two types of paradigms: the *paradigm of oneness,* the belief that God and the individual are one, and the *paradigm of separation,* the belief that God and the individual are separate. As we'll see, while there are no variations in the paradigm of oneness, the paradigm of separation takes many different forms, a few of which I'll mention here.

It may seem odd to say that every person's paradigm includes some understanding of God. What about the atheist who declares there is no God? How can a thing that, to them does not exist, impact their life? The belief in no God affects the way atheists see everything, especially themselves. Their opinions about things like religion, culture, science, and the purpose of the individual will be different from those who believe God exists. The atheist will likely attribute their existence to biology and brain function. Their paradigm of separation influences everything from the kinds of books they read, to the political candidate they support or denounce, to which items in the news grab their attention, to the types people they consider friends. Every aspect of their life conforms perfectly to their paradigm of separation.

On the other end is the religious fundamentalist who thinks of God as being up in the heavens looking down on humanity. There is a strong belief in God, but an equally strong belief that God and the individual are separate. This paradigm of separation, though different from that of the atheist, also affects the way they view everything from politics to individual purpose.

Probably the most subtle version of the paradigm of separation manifests within the New Thought Movement, specifically as the notion of the evolving soul. This movement declares all people are one with God, but in practice we see a lot of looking to the future for the dawn of a new age, the healing of the planet, the coming of world peace, or the tipping the balance toward a collectively evolving Christ consciousness. Declaring God and I are here but the manifestations of the fruits of oneness have not yet arrived represents a paradigm of separation.

Whether we consider the beliefs of a self-proclaimed atheist, the spiritual convictions of the deeply religious, or the theology of an entire religious denomination (New Thought or Traditional), discern the paradigm each holds, and you have the key to understanding why they believe and/or teach as they do. You have an understanding of Truth as they see it.

But is it *the* Truth? If, as Wheeler believed, the existence of the universe (the universe of each individual in particular), requires an observer, then the basis from which we make our observations determines the nature and tone of our reality. The paradigm we hold *is* the truth of our universe. If a thing does not fit our paradigm, we reject it. If it does fit, we accept it. There is no power that compels us to embrace our paradigm. Nor is there a power that coerces us into letting it go. There is only the logical outworking, the consequence of the paradigm we embrace as truth. From our perspective, apart from the paradigm we adopt, there is no absolute Truth. We accept the consequences of our core beliefs as the natural outworking of truth as we understand it. If we don't like what we see, we seek to bring it into alignment with our truth through the rules dictated by our paradigm.

But again, is this *the* Truth just because we say it is? Is there not a standard of reality beyond our personal perception? Before we answer this question, let's revisit Cady's ocean illustration. Rather than using the ocean and her pail, the ocean and a sponge will work better here.

Imagine immersing the sponge in the ocean. The paradigm of oneness depicts the ocean as the single living reality, the omnipresence that permeates and enlivens the sponge. Though there is water inside and outside the sponge, the water itself remains one substance. Think of the soul as that water circulating within the parameters of the sponge, and God as the entire ocean. There is no point where the water outside of the sponge becomes something different from the water on the inside. Even if you squeeze out the water and toss the sponge, the water is unaffected. A statement of being for this paradigm of oneness might go something like this: *I am an eternal soul, one with the infinite sea of life (ocean), localized and expressing through this body (sponge).*

In contrast, like our earlier analogy involving the pail, the paradigm of separation focuses on the sponge as the primary anchor of the individual's identity. The ocean is *out there*, a thing different from the sponge. Even the water within the sponge is something different. We saw this in our Spirit (ocean), soul (water within the sponge), and body (sponge) model. Rather than thinking of the soul as water circulating through the sponge, this paradigm holds that the sponge has, somewhere in its depths, this mysterious water called a soul that is either in need of evolving or salvation. The focus of the self-image is the sponge itself. The statement of being for this paradigm might go like this: *I am a body-based self-image (sponge) containing this mysterious element called a soul, in a vast ocean (God) that surrounds me.*

If each of these paradigms represents Truth to the one who holds them, how is it possible to determine Truth in the absolute sense? Jesus gave us an important key when he said, "… *you will know the truth and the truth will make you free.*"[71] The operative word here is *know*. The standard of Truth we take from this statement is the *experience of freedom.* When you *know* Truth, Jesus is saying, you experience freedom.

If the experience of freedom is the key, then how are we to understand the meaning of freedom in this context? Like anyone living in a relatively free society, the Jews took exception to Jesus' statement by saying, "*We are descendants of Abraham, and have never been in bondage to any one. How is it that you say, 'You will be made free?'*"[72]

In this illustration, we are considering the two elements of water and the sponge, both of which offer important clues on how we might think of freedom in a spiritual context. Water is indestructible but the sponge is not. If we stretch our imagination a bit, we can say that water, because of its indestructibility, has nothing to fear. The sponge, on the other hand, is subject to a whole range of potentially destructive elements.

Because the soul, like water, is indestructible, it knows nothing

[71] John 8:32
[72] John 8:33

of fear. *"For God has not given us a spirit of fear, but of power and of love and of a sound mind."*[73] The self-image, on the other hand, is forever guarding its endless list of weaknesses.

Everyone has anxious moments, but if we experience a steady stream of anxiety, if our body is tied in knots, our sense of self, as we saw in Chapter 1, has migrated away from the soul and fallen under the influence of the body-based self-image. We've shifted our understanding of who we are from the water to the sponge. The water in the sponge, one with the ocean, does not look forward to a time when it will be free of fear. It has nothing to fear now.

The Paradigm of Oneness

The paradigm of oneness most accurately represents the universal Truth that sets us free. This paradigm rests on the foundation of the omnipresence of God expressing as the complete soul, our spiritual essence that, grounded in our eternal source, is both indestructible and free. When you experience the Truth of your soul, you experience the epitome of freedom.

This ocean/sponge illustration, then, provides an excellent basis for discussion of the trinity of core values that I'm calling the paradigm of oneness. Thinking of God as the ocean and the water within the sponge as the soul, we see instantly the indivisible relationship between God and the soul. What the illustration does not reveal is an understanding of the nature of God, which is where we begin in our exploration of this paradigm.

The Nature of God

God, the omnipresent Creative Life Force, is universal consciousness, the underlying life, love, power, and intelligence that is the cause of all things.

I find that thinking of God as the Creative Life Force makes it somewhat easier to resist the temptation to assign human characteristics to our universal Source. Each of us, endowed with the insatiable desire to be free, can trace this impulse for freedom to that ever-expanding fountain of living energy to which we owe our existence. We desire freedom because, at the soul level, we are

---

[73] 2 Timothy 1:7, New King James Version

free already.

God achieves perpetual diversification through the process of individualizing as the soul of every living thing. The desire and the ability to carry on this limitless expansion are natural endowments that all life forms share in common. We restrict this natural expansive process by assigning God human moods, attitudes, and motives that can be influenced, positively or negatively, by our actions. Thinking of God as the infinite ocean of pure Being, in which, as Paul wrote, "... *we live and move and have our being. . .,*"[74] is one helpful way of doing this. The sponge immersed in the ocean can never alter the unconditional presence or nature of the ocean.

Emile Cady gave another excellent way to think of God as Being rather than God as *a being:*

> God is not a being or person having life, intelligence, love, power. God is that invisible, intangible, but very real, something we call life. God is perfect love and infinite power. God is the total of these, the total of all good, whether manifested or unexpressed.[75]

The Psalmist gave a more poetic way of expanding our thinking of God into the broader context of omnipresence:

> "Whither shall I go from thy Spirit? Or whither shall I flee from thy presence? If I ascend to heaven, thou art there! If I make my bed in Sheol, thou art there! If I take the wings of the morning and dwell in the uttermost parts of the sea, even there thy hand shall lead me, and thy right hand shall hold me."[76]

As Being, God is the living foundation that underlies and supports all aspects of the universe. Just as white light contains the full spectrum of color, so this divine foundation consists of the four fundamentals of life, love, power, and intelligence. We can think of the sum of these as universal, or, as some scientists are now calling it, *nonlocalized consciousness.* Imbued with this consciousness, all creatures utilize and express it according to their

---

[74] Acts 17:28
[75] Lessons in Truth
[76] Psalms 139:7-10

biological capacities. This variation of expression gives the impression of multiple levels of consciousness, but all living things derive their being from the same, universal Source.

To understand this, think of the sun shining through various sized windows. This single light source appears as differing degrees of manifestation, but the light passing through a window of any size is the same as that which engulfs the entire building.

The current scientific model, of course, does not acknowledge Being as a preexistent foundation out of which all expressions of life arise. It takes the opposite position that life somehow spontaneously combusted out of matter, that sunlight mysteriously originates at the window. Despite the advancement of multiple theories on how life might have risen from matter, none proves true in the laboratory. The assumption that matter produced life raises the simple question of why this is not happening still. Are we to assume this occurrence is so rare that it only happened once in earth's 4.6 billion year history?

Science never seems to tire of elbowing religion for its endorsement of the Biblical six days of creation. Yet it goes to great lengths to convince the world that all matter and subsequent life exploded from a single subatomic particle to our entire universe in a millionth of a millionth of a millionth of a millionth of a millisecond. I have no doubt that the big bang, as some forward-thinking scientists are predicting, is destined to become the flat earth of our time. I do not believe that science is likely to utter, *in the beginning God,* but I do think it will envision a beginning that allows the material to rise from a pre-existent foundation of universal consciousness, not the other way around.

The Nature of the Individual: God individualizes as the soul and self-awareness of each person. The fundamentals of life, love, power, and intelligence express as the individual soul.

Returning to our window analogy, we can think of the sun's light on the outside of the building as God and that same light passing through the window as the soul. As you know by now, the basic premise of this book is that the soul of every individual, like the light shining through the window, is complete and has always been complete. If we turn to the familiar first five verses of John and take the liberty of substituting *Word* with *soul,* as I think we may do, we'll see this is not a new concept:

> In the beginning was the soul, and the soul was with God, and the soul was God. The soul was in the beginning with God; all things were made through the soul, and without the soul was not anything made that was made. In the soul was life, and the life was the light of men. The light shines in the darkness, and the darkness has not overcome it.

The soul, existing in a present dimension untouched by time and space, is the funneled down expression of universal consciousness to individual consciousness, self-awareness. As such, the soul exists in the eternal now, predating even the most primitive biological forms. Though the soul is able to express through any material environment capable of supporting a physical host, it remains fully intact whether or not a biologically sustainable environment is available. What we see in terms of human development is really an evolution of the brain and body, the soul's physical interface. We do not see an evolution of the soul that has always been, as John points out, *"in the beginning with God."*

The Relationship Between God and the Individual: The relationship between God and the individual soul is absolute oneness. There are no natural barriers, no lines of demarcation between God and the individual soul.

The light outside the building represents God. The light streaming through the window represents God expressing or individualizing as the soul. Likewise, the water of the ocean and the water within the sponge immersed in the ocean are one.

Speaking of God *and* the soul implies duality, but this is a limitation in language only. John tried to resolve this language barrier by writing, *"the Word was with God, and the Word was God."* Still, the temptation is to think of two things, God *and* the Word, or God *and* the soul, rather than seeing these as a single power expressing both in a universal and individualized manner. We find a similar attempt to resolve the problem in this variously attributed quote: *"God is a circle whose center is everywhere and circumference nowhere"* (Voltaire, Pascal, Empedocles ...). One of the best ways of saying it is that there is no point where God leaves off and the soul begins.

Contrasting the Paradigms

Several biblical illustrations present a clear contrast between the paradigms of oneness and separation. We find one of the best examples in the fifth chapter of John[77] involving a man who, for thirty-eight years, lay ill beside a pool said to have healing properties. When the waters were "troubled," presumably by divine forces, the first person to make it into the water would be healed.

When Jesus spotted the man, he said to him, *"Do you want to be healed?"* The man explained, *"Sir, I have no man to put me into the pool when the water is troubled, and while I am going another steps down before me."*

The man holds the paradigm of separation, the belief that there is a time-space barrier between him and his desired healing. Jesus, acting out of the paradigm of oneness, said to him, *"Rise, take up your pallet, and walk."* In other words, Jesus was telling the man there were no barriers to healing. To the man's surprise, the solution was present and had been present all along. The man experienced an immediate paradigm shift, for he stood, took up his bed, and walked.

Point A and Point B

As we've seen, the spiritual evolutionist attempts to merge the tenets of science and spirituality by placing the soul on a time-line more fitting to biological evolution. Adopting this view we think of the soul and our current condition in life as being at an imaginary Point A. We're that partially filled pail that is gradually working its way to Point B, that state of illumination we envision as our destination. This is our pail completely full. The process of moving from Point A to Point B is considered the spiritual path required to successfully fulfill our soul's destiny.

We navigate this path based on our perception of the distance between where we are right now (Point A) and where we think we need to be (Point B). Our spiritual path becomes our plan of resolution, our route to closing the gap by navigating through, around, or over perceived barriers, and reaching the spiritual ideal we seek.

---

[77] John 5:1-10

I have noticed that while many consider themselves firmly committed to making progress on this path, few actually believe they are nearing their ultimate vision of perfection. They may consider it progress to make the mental shift from seeing their pail as half empty to seeing it from the more optimistic, half full. It may make them feel better, but they are still left with their Point A and Point B model with all that distance in between.

This was the perspective I tried to reconcile the entire time I lived as a soul evolutionist. Like many, I adopted the *earth as school* approach. This required the concerted effort of applying spiritual insights to the various challenges that life presented. Where I may have once reacted to the cutting words of another, I could see myself making gradual progress toward letting such words pass without internalizing them in the usual peace-robbing way. Or, rather than fall into a state of fear and panic over some loss or perceived threat, I could more quickly gather my spiritual wits and affirm the greater good unfolding through this unwanted situation. My growing level of nonresistance to negative people and appearances seemed the type of promising evidence characteristic of an evolving soul. But this approach was slow, fraught with relapses and, frankly, very discouraging. My truth, I came to realize, was apparently not *the* Truth.

Another aspect of this problem is the belief that my life as it is (Point A), is inadequate, that I must reach some material or spiritual objective (Point B) before it will be fulfilling. Again, the seeming remedy is to add more knowledge and rise to a new level of consciousness that will manifest as a more prosperous life.

This Point A/Point B paradigm of separation assumes the condition we believe will bring us completeness exists in some future development or acquisition. There are a couple of significant problems with this approach, particularly as it pertains to the spiritual path. First, as long as there is a Point A—seeing yourself separated from your ideal—there will always be a Point B. The distance between the two *never* closes. You may be absolutely correct in your assessment that your Point A has moved three feet in a positive direction. You may feel more optimism toward your life. But when you truly look at it, you will see your Point B has moved three feet down that path as well. Every new revelation simply starts the process all over. You're kicking the spiritual can down the road.

Two Magnets

You can see this dynamic illustrated by placing two disk magnets side by side on a table with their poles opposing. Push Magnet A toward Magnet B and Magnet B will move away. Where on the table can you slide Magnet A to make it more attractive to Magnet B? No place. As long as the two poles of the magnets remain in opposition, you can move them anywhere and they will continue to repel one another. Flip over one magnet and the two will snap together at any location. Neither the nature of the magnets nor their physical placement needs to change. To make the magnets attractive to each other, reverse their poles and they will snap together wherever they are.

So it is with us. The paradigm of separation is the polar opposite to the paradigm of oneness. What we must flip over in ourselves is not the condition of our soul but rather our trinity of core values. Our paradigm of oneness model, then, takes the following form: Point A/B

This model holds that our present environment is God and our present soul condition is whole and one with God. This, I believe, is what Jesus was trying to explain when he said,

> "Do you not say, 'There are yet four months, then comes the harvest'? I tell you, lift up your eyes, and see how the fields are already white for harvest."[78]

The Elusive Now

From the point of view of the self-image, the future and the past, time and space, present major barriers. From the soul's perspective, these things are nonexistent. Yes, there is that moment when life in the pail on the beach began. But the soul has no beginning.

The idea that time is an illusion appeals to the self-image enslaved to it. When we learn that now is the only time, that fearing the future and regretting the past drain our spiritual power, the self-image quickly constructs a new concept that it labels *the now moment*. While it is true that this moment is the only one we will ever have, attempting to conceptualize it as a memory file is as futile as fabricating a boat of paper. Place this boat in water, climb aboard,

---

[78] John 4:35

and shove off your shore. You'll find the clock ticks louder and faster than ever.

Though the self-image finds the concept intriguing, it cannot conceive of the eternal now as having anything of practical value. Everything we do at the level of the self-image is measured in relation to time and space. As we've seen, the self-image has placed the soul's evolution on a linear scale that is incompatible with the now moment. We simply cannot merge our concepts of time and eternity in a manner applicable to our daily routine.

Only the soul understands the eternal environment of the now moment. It is not fettered with the task of releasing the notions of past and future and grasping an idea foreign to its being. Your soul has never known anything other than the freedom of the eternal now.

As you acknowledge and allow your soul to emerge into your awareness, it establishes its own environment in and as your consciousness. At the soul level, you do not embrace a concept like the now moment just because it has become popular or even because it seems logical. You come to know the now moment as a fact of your soul. Your completeness is not two or even one step ahead of where your soul resides. It is not necessary to try and grasp this. Just accept that the experience of the eternal now is among the many freeing revelations that your soul brings to your surface awareness. You have no beginning, you have no end. Your soul will not one day knock and ask that you open the door. It is knocking now.

Opening the door to our soul is the infilling. Expressing our gifts to the world is the other side of our creative endeavor. In the next chapter we will look at the natural faculties we use to express our soul in meaningful and productive ways.

CHAPTER 8

OUR EXECUTIVE FACULTIES

As part of its consciousness-forming equipment, the soul has at its disposal five faculties with which to work. I refer to them as *executive faculties* because we can make a deliberate choice as to how we will use them. Our choice will either strengthen our self-image or it will contribute to building the interface through which the soul may express and interact with the material realm. We use these both consciously and unconsciously. By listing them and discussing how each one works, we become more aware of how we are using them.

There are five executive faculties. They are *imagination, faith, will, judgment,* and *elimination.* If you are familiar with Charles Fillmore's *Twelve Powers of Man,* you will see some overlap in the terminology I use here. You will also see some stark contrasts, five rather than twelve faculties, for example. Limiting the group to five rather than twelve is not an effort to coordinate with the five senses or to update or otherwise change the Fillmorian *twelve-power* model. I am simply presenting a model that is better suited to my understanding of prayer and our spiritual objective of expressing the soul.

Whether we are thinking in terms of using these faculties toward spiritual transformation, or we are simply going through our typical routine of daily living, we use all five at all times. When the self-image employs these faculties, they are always directed to external conditions, usually with the intention of invoking some level of the *law of attraction*. The motive for making a special effort to invoke this law usually involves strengthening, protecting, and in some way advancing the senses-based agenda of the self-image. When these same faculties are employed by the soul, it is always in conjunction with the *law of expression*. Our purpose is to advance or express the soul's inherent qualities of life, love, power and intelligence. The self-image is a taker, forever seeking light and sustenance from outside sources. The soul is a giver and will always let its light shine from within. The law of expression automatically invokes the law of attraction.

The soul needs no instruction on how to use these five faculties. Unlike the self-image, the soul does not employ them as a means of building and fortifying its being. Their usage comes as natural to us as the heartbeat and the breath to the body. In our conscious return to the soul, we do find that we need to be mindful of how we are employing these faculties. How we use them depends on whether or not we have truly *come to ourselves* and experienced a genuine shift in our core values. Are we merely running away from pain, or do we understand the value of the spiritual homecoming? This is one area where we cannot mask a disingenuous motivation. Though the world remains unaware of our innermost intentions, spiritually inauthentic motives are like clouds that block the soul's light. No one but us can see these clouds, and nothing less than our sincere desire to reconnect with our soul can cause them to dissipate.

The executive faculties make up what we might think of as a tool-kit of prayer, a subject we'll explore in greater depth in the final chapter of this book. The following is a general summary of these faculties, an overview that should familiarize you with how we will be thinking of them and their roles in both the meditative and prayer processes.

Imagination

> "The eye is the lamp of the body. So, if your eye is sound, your whole body will be full of light; but if your eye is not sound, your whole body will be full of darkness. If then the light in you is darkness, how great is the darkness!"[79]

Because of its direct influence on the quality of our life, the first and most important of the executive faculties is that of the imagination. Also known as the mind's eye, we normally think of the imagination only as the visualizing aspect, that ability to form pictures and sensations independent of the five senses. We will find it useful to expand this understanding by thinking of the imagination as a single faculty embodying both intellectual and intuitive functions.

The intellectual function is the more familiar side we know as the picture-forming, logic-based, rational mind. Because this aspect is prone to *reductionism*, the belief that all complex systems can be understood by breaking them down to their individual components, it relies on information it can see, hear, touch, taste, and smell. With this function, we build a consciousness and a worldview based on information gleaned through the five senses, either directly, with the expanded help of technology, or through theoretical assumption.

The intuitive function, on the other hand, is our means of acquiring knowledge of our spiritual makeup without inference or obvious facts. It is our portal to the unseen reality of the soul. The intuitive function should not be thought of as *a sixth sense*, as in extra sensory perception, but as a faculty designed specifically for bringing the soul's influence into our field of awareness. When this faculty is opened, the intuition begins to play a significant role in our daily decision making, even to the point of tipping the scale away from our usual dominating intellectual evaluations.

Emilie Cady described it in this way: *"Intuition and intellect are meant to travel together, intuition always holding the reins to guide intellect."* I do not believe she was implying that our growing spiritual awareness causes us to use the intellect less. She is simply saying we will naturally use our intuitive faculty more. Information the intuition brings rises from what is true of the soul. From this we build our consciousness and worldview. Our mental imagery is influenced by this internal resource, the original spring of our being that is who and what we are at this deepest level. The consciousness and the body become instruments of the soul, the soul's interactive interface to the material realm.

Those people in whom these faculties are heavy on either the intellectual or intuitive end of the scale, will tend to hold completely differing views of themselves and the world. When the consciousness is weighted toward the objective mind, we get the intellectual, the scientific reductionist, the academic philosopher, and the atheist who must fit the essence of the human being into the confines of the brain. When the consciousness is weighted toward the subjective mind, we get the mystic, the artist, the intuitive scientist, and the spiritual philosopher who assumes the soul utilizes the brain as a transmitter. When the consciousness leans slightly toward the intellect from center, we might see an Albert Einstein, an intuitively inspired intellectual genius who openly stated, *"All great achievements of science must start from intuitive knowledge."* When the consciousness leans slightly more to the intuitive from center, we may see an Emerson, an intellectually astute, spiritual genius who recognized, *"Every man is the inlet, and may become the outlet, to all there is in God."* With the consciousness balanced, we get a Jesus Christ. *"... that you may know and understand that the Father is in me and I am in the Father."*[80]

Those attempting to create the perfect self-image upon which a successful, fulfilling material, and spiritual life can be built, labor under the false notion that they can accomplish this through the visualizing aspect of the imagination only. Using such tools as vision boards and positive affirmations, they attempt to create the self-image attractive to wealth and success. Regardless of how shining and air-tight this self-image may seem, if the consciousness is not grounded in the soul, they are boarding a rudderless ship that will forever remain adrift seeking a harbor it can never reach.

The intuitive portal, never fully closed, allows just enough of the soul's light to shine through to create a beacon. We sense that our disappointment with acquisitions and accomplishments is but a call to look beyond or beneath externals for that which genuinely satisfies. This beacon is at first a misinterpreted, vague unrest, a gnawing dissatisfaction that indicates our search for stability and lasting peace must ultimately turn from the outer and become inner directed.

As we have seen, the journey of the *I* is from the intellectually based self-image to the intuitively based inner sanctuary of the soul. Once there, we may leave home, but never without the awareness that we have done so. A conscience that was once grounded in culturally based moral standards is now gradually moved to its true

---

[80] John 10:38

spiritual baseline. We graduate from *thou shall not* out of fear of reprisal for disobeying a capricious God, to the purer *thou shall not*, simply because our true nature is incapable of engaging in spiritually degrading behavior. Once we touch this center, we are more aware, often painfully so, when we stray. This problem is unknown to those who regard the self-image and its prodigal, far-country milieu as their permanent home. These types attempt to live by the commandments posted in stone. The soul, on the other hand, finds its rules of conduct written into its very constitution.

As we still the senses-based intellect and turn the reins over to the intuition, we are gradually led to the inner sanctum of the soul. Once we connect with this foundation, and we know it when we do, the intuitive aspect of the imagination feeds its visualizing counterpart to become the outlet, the interfacing consciousness through which the soul expresses and interacts with the material plane.

Faith

> "Whoever says to this mountain, 'be taken up and cast into the sea,' and does not doubt in his heart, but believes that what he says will come to pass, it will be done for him. Therefore I tell you, whatever you ask in prayer, believe that you have received it, and it will be yours."[81]

The second executive faculty is that of faith. Like all of these faculties, we need to consider faith from the dual perspectives of the soul and the self-image. From the soul's point of view, faith is that ever-expansive urge for greater freedom we observe in ourselves and in all life forms. It pushes the seedling up through the safety of the soil into a different and much broader world. It nudges the fledgling eagle to launch from its nest-centered universe and invoke laws of flight that, until that critical moment, lay dormant. Our soul's inherent faith expresses as the assurance that the necessary supply and conditions required to support our sojourn into the material dimension are forthcoming. Faith is a word we apply to the soul's intrinsic knowing that our needs will be met, our journey successful, come what may. The writer of

---

[81] Mark 11:23-24

Hebrews defined faith as *the substance of things hoped for, the evidence of things not seen.*[82]

Another way to think of faith is to see it as our level of *expectation*, though not necessarily for a specific outcome: *I just know my horse is going to win this time.* Our focus is on the overall tendency of our life. Is my expectation for the greater good unfolding through my life or do I expect things to move on a downward trend? Even if your horse loses the race, your life can still be on an upward trend that in all ways reflects the tendency toward ever-greater freedom.

Our faculty of faith is that inner prompting, that still small voice[83] that calls us home; it is the force that prompts the migration of our self-awareness from the far country of the self-image to its rightful place in the soul. The single objective of faith becomes the experience of the soul. The prodigal began his return home with extremely low expectations, faith small as a mustard seed. The power of his demonstration lay not in the understanding of what life would be like upon his return, but in his singleness of purpose for returning. He had the faith to take that first step, blind and as uncertain as it was.

"The journey of a thousand miles begins with a single step."
— *Lao Tzu*

Lao Tzu was obviously calling attention to the importance and simplicity of a single action, the repetition of which holds the power to broaden the horizon of virtually anyone. So it is with faith. In the prodigal's case, his expectation was not in receiving robes, rings, and banquets in his honor. He wanted the freedom from fear that only his return home could give. This is what we all want. Our longing for a more prosperous, freedom-filled life is really a deep yearning to make a conscious connection with our soul, our true home. The satisfaction we once thought was obtainable only through accomplishments and possessions, we now understand resides in our spiritual depths.

Returning to the home of our soul does not mean a forfeiture of material desires. Our experience in the quiet domain of this spiritually authentic level provides the needed insight to know

[82] Hebrews 11:1
[83] 1 Kings 19:12

when we are attempting to derive from the material that which only the soul can give. This brings clarity to the idea of faith as the substance of things hoped for. What we're hoping for, what we are expecting, the very substance we are seeking with our acquisitions, is the greater experience of life, love, power and intelligence and all the peace and freedom these imply.

Will

> "Thy kingdom come. Thy will be done, On earth as it is in heaven."[84]

The third executive faculty is that of will. In the context of the soul, the meaning of will aligns with volition, the commitment to a particular course of action and direction, and the *willingness* to allow for this or something better. The will of your soul, having taken on a body and committed to expressing through the experience of the material plane is now being done.

From the point of view of our spiritual homecoming, the will is the faculty that allows us to change our previous course and then keep our every step pointed in the direction of our newly conceived freedom. We exercise the faculty of will as our means of keeping the intuitive portal open, the picturing aspect of the imagination properly focused, and our faith directed to spiritual wholeness.

We also exercise our will when we reign in negative thinking and emotion carried away by challenging appearances. We become willing to look beyond immediate circumstances, and consider different possibilities. The soul has but one desire, and that is its commitment to freedom, expression without limits. Our desire to reconnect with the soul is prompted by this call of freedom. *Let thy will be done,* then, is the highest form of prayer when directed to the soul. Follow this with the acknowledgment that *thy will is being done, on earth* (in expression) *as it is in heaven* (the unseen realm of the soul).

---

[84] Matthew 6:10

Chapter 8

Judgment

> "Again, the kingdom of heaven is like a net which was thrown into the sea and gathered fish of every kind; when it was full, men drew it ashore and sat down and sorted the good into vessels but threw away the bad."[85]

Our fourth executive faculty is judgment. The fact that there are no natural barriers to the soul's expression and no opposition to its creative endeavors means that our faculty of judgment is naturally biased toward all possibility. In our return to the soul, the faculty of judgment rests in a single question: Does the thing under consideration advance the cause of our spiritual homecoming, or does it prolong it? The belief in the evolving soul hinders our homecoming. It serves as a perpetual detour sign suggesting that a longer route must be taken because our soul is still under development.

Because there are no natural barriers, no detours between our self-awareness and our rightful home of the soul, we employ our faculty of judgment to see past appearances of perceived blockages. The apparent detours we formerly considered as providing needed lessons for our soul's advancement are now seen as false perceptions, impotent in their ability to continue representing distance between where we are and where we want to be. There is no series of steps, no crutches, no help from outside sources needed to reach the healing pool of spiritual enlightenment. We hold to the truth that now is the acceptable time to take up our bed and walk. We may take side roads, for example, and become preoccupied with outer conditions that seem capable of advancing our journey when these do little more than keep us confined to our bed of limitation.

There is a substantial sector of the spiritual community that perceives our faculty of judgment as a hindrance to be denied if we are to advance. We are not to eliminate judgment, but employ it under the guidance of the soul. The self-image judges according to appearances based on self-advancement and self-preservation. Its judgment always involves the protection of some weakness. In its highest form of expression, the faculty of judgment provides our

[85] Matthew 13:47-48

ability to discern the difference between protecting a weakness of the self-image and advancing the strength of the soul. Are we responding to the promptings of the self-image or are we motivated by the urging of the soul? If we are protecting a weakness of the self-image, then we are residing at the level of the self-image. The consequence is our perception of life from a level that assures continued struggle.

As the fishermen in the above parable used judgment to discern between the good fish and the bad, so we must keep this important faculty intact, that we may discern the difference between what is true of the soul, and toss back the false evaluations that originate with the self-image. This ability to identify and release those ideas that keep our spiritual awakening on a perpetual detour brings us to our final executive faculty: *elimination*.

Elimination

> "And if any one will not receive you or listen to your words, shake off the dust from your feet as you leave that house or town."[86]

> And he said to them, "Follow me, and I will make you fishers of men." Immediately they left their nets and followed him.[87]

In addition to these sayings, the parables of the dragnet and of the hidden treasure are as much about elimination as they are about acquisition. The soul is not plagued with a need to hang onto spiritual maxims and any other thing it considers valuable. The soul itself is of the highest value and it finds no need to cling to anything less. The struggling self-image, on the other hand, has placed great value on many things it considers essential to its survival. An emerging, spiritually-based value system poses constant challenges to the materially-centered ego. In the man's selling of his possessions, he did it in great joy because he first saw the value of the newly discovered treasure. The rich young ruler had never seen this treasure and would likely not have recognized its value even if he had. To him, the acquisition of eternal life was nothing more than a concept, an appealing idea that would allow

[86] Matthew 10:14
[87] Matthew 4:19-20

him to remain in his self-image and relish his earthly treasures forever. A true understanding of eternal life involves a genuine interest in the nature of the soul. It was the rich man's true love of things that would not allow him to break free from the orbit of his self-image's gravitational pull.

As the light of the soul begins to dawn on us, we joyously release attachments to those materially centered ideas that interfere with the growing awareness of our true spiritual home. Because it is the value we place on a thing, rather than the thing itself, that binds us, there is no official list of distractions, no seven deadly sins, no absolute roster of things to be avoided. Reading spiritually-based material can become as much of a distraction to a direct experience of the soul as can the effects of becoming a news junkie. When we feel the distracting power or the unnecessary weight of a thing that prompts a non-resolvable preoccupation with any issue, we let it go.

We learn that we should be more loving, for example, and so we try to love those who may not be so lovable. As itself an expression of love, the soul does not need this instruction. Love is a fundamental of the soul regardless of what others do or fail to do. The more we experience our spiritual depths, the more loving we become. Our understanding of love shifts from a verb, a thing we do, to a noun, a fundamental quality of our being. As Emilie Cady points out, we want "... *a love that will not have to be pumped up by a determined effort because we know that it is right to love and wrong not to love, but a love that will flow with the spontaneity and fullness of an artesian well ...*"[88]

There is no need to muster the will to force the light of love to shine, when our natural being allows us to simply let it shine.[89]

This letting is an important shift in understanding. When the soul forms consciousness, it does so purely from the standpoint of self expression. As the writer of Hebrews acknowledged, the things that we see are made from things invisible to the naked eye.[90] The soul externalizes first as the equivalent in consciousness of that which already exists at the soul level. This consciousness then serves as the basis or blueprint which the now obedient intellect uses as its guide to translate this blueprint into equivalent material

---

[88] Lessons In Truth
[89] Matthew 5:16
[90] Hebrews 11:3

conditions.

Pairs of Opposites

According to the Gospel writers, Jesus often made his points by comparing pairs of opposites. We see good fish and bad fish, God and mammon, wheat and chaff, rich man and poor man, sheep and goats, foolish virgins and wise virgins, the wide gate and narrow gate, born of the flesh and born of the spirit, foundation of rock and foundation of sand, and so on. In every instance, we can think of the comparisons as relating to the self-image and the soul.

In his parable of the prodigal son, the opposites are depicted in the actions of leaving and returning home. Leaving home is the story of the self-image while returning is the story of the soul. It is worth noting that leaving and returning uses the same path, but moving in opposite directions. Both in his leaving and in his return, the young man employs all five executive faculties, but for exactly opposite purposes. On his way out, we can see him utilizing only the visualizing side of the imagination. Like a skilled novelist, he generates a fictional, financially irresponsible, and sexually promiscuous character that he drops onto the stage of an equally fictional worldview. His faith is in the money in his pocket. His will is turned totally on self-gratification. His judgment is tainted with desire. He essentially eliminates his ties to home and his sense of responsibility to his true character.

The story reaches a pivotal moment when the young man, destitute and nearly starved, comes to himself. Prior to this moment, all his decisions are made to strengthen, advance and even protect the self-image. Once he hits bottom, he becomes willing to make decisions based on the deeper promptings of the soul. *I'm not this*, he says of his shallow life. *I'm something more.* The moment he comes to himself represents the opening of the imagination's intuitive portal. The law of attraction has performed perfectly in mirroring a transient world of affairs equal in its shallowness to his own self-image. In this moment of truth, the law of expression takes over and the journey home begins. Now the law of attraction draws the supply needed to make his every step one that takes him that much closer to home.

We may wonder how the self-image could possibly fabricate and inhabit such a false understanding of the world. Not all that long ago people were quite comfortable with the geocentric model that placed earth at the orbital center of all celestial bodies. One could be punished with death for thinking otherwise. The Age of Enlightenment, with its advancement of correct intellectual reason, did not return our planet to its proper place. The earth had never strayed. This long held belief that the sun, moon, planets and stars revolved around the earth was never a fact of nature. It was nothing more than a tenaciously held, false perception residing in the collective imagination of an extremely persuasive but astronomically ignorant clergy. The earth *had* to reside at the center to make their perception of the cosmos work. Apparently no one told the cosmos.

When long held tenets of our personal worldview are shattered and our faith in a limited version of reality is pushed well beyond its limits, it is more likely that the intuitive portal of the imagination will open. In our humility, we are much more receptive to the emergence of an entirely different version of reality. When things are going well, when we are headed into the far country with a pocket full of cash, we don't have the same urgency or willingness to come to ourselves in a soul-searching quest for truth as we would in a moment of crisis.

I'm not suggesting that we need a crisis to wake up to our spiritual side. But when the self-image's best-laid plans begin to unravel, the likelihood of our deeper probing increases. This is especially true if we have been in pursuit of a genuine understanding of spiritual matters. As I said, we can get two completely different views traveling on the same road, depending on which direction we are going. Likewise, we can have two completely different worldviews depending on whether we are traveling out to the far country or returning home. This, I believe, is what Jesus encountered in the following exchange:

> Again he said to them, "I go away, and you will seek me and die in your sin; where I am going, you cannot come." Then said the Jews, "Will he kill himself, since he says, 'Where I am going, you cannot come'?" He said to them, "You are from below, I am from above; you are of this world, I am not of this world."[91]

---

[91] John 8:21-23

Though Jesus and this group of Jews met at a common place in the road, they were traveling in two completely different directions, guided by two different sets of values. One was headed to the far country, the other was headed home. I think of this exchange as the soul addressing the self-image. Where I am going, you cannot come. You are from below [realm of the senses] I am from above [spiritual dimension]; you are of this world, I am not of this world. In other words, there are two very distinct ways of experiencing this life in a body. Both involve the issue of supply, a very important topic we will explore next.

CHAPTER 9

NATURAL SUPPLY

Our prodigal awareness, forever trolling the reef-laden shallows of the material domain, never quite forgets that our real home has no shores. We sit in the safety of the harbor with our books, our teachers and our sacred scriptures. We visit the beach, gaze in reverence and wonder into that mist-shrouded horizon that stirs in us a strange mix of mystery and primordial familiarity. With our values, our house and our affairs orderly and firmly established in harbor life, we think a certain way, the starting point always from these surrounding beaches. We contemplate and read about the sea and we seek to reconcile the fact that we are so deeply moved by this boundless vista, this restless living thing that stirs before us.

Then, at some unexpected moment, a profound revelation breaks into our awareness. Our house may indeed stand in the harbor, our ship, safely moored at the pier, but our true home is the open sea. This incessant longing that keeps bringing us back to the wonder we behold from this beach, to the feel of cool waves washing over our feet, is that completed part of us that never has and never shall leave the unconditional freedom of this eternal sea. To know this truth and to value it above all is to put our heart in the Truth that makes us free.

– JDB

As we've seen, one of the restrictions we encounter with a body is its care and maintenance. Yet when Matthew included Jesus' discourse on the lilies of the field and the birds of the air, he did so in a way that suggests a condition where the body is supplied by something transcending the usual sweat-of-the-brow approach to meeting our material needs. He may have been hinting at this with Nicodemus when he pointed out the need to be born anew, to dislodge focus on the body-centered self-image and move the awareness back to its rightful place ... the soul. Might this have been why he also said, *"And call no man your father on earth, for you have one Father, who is in heaven."*[92] Is he not calling attention to our true being as spiritual rather than biological?

Extended Dependence as Infants

Of all living creatures, we humans take the prize when it comes to extended dependence in infancy. Unless we were fortunate enough to be born to parents who did not confuse our soul with our body (this would be a cultural rarity), we have much to learn, not in the way of soul education, but in bodily disassociation. While in the womb, we took no thought of hunger, warmth, and security. The instant we emerged from this all-sustaining incubator, any absence of these accustomed comforts suddenly became a factor. We were, for the first time, introduced to the reality of lack. In addition, people took the place of the womb in providing our physical comforts and essentials.

It was during this critical phase of infancy that our life of service to the needs of the body began. The culture into which we were born inadvertently lured us into the hope that we could draw permanent sustenance and satisfaction from the material world. In the eyes of some, competition for resources began *a cognitive arms race*, as one evolutionary biologist describes it.[93] We experienced the nakedness of lack and decided we would do most anything to avoid it. Possession-based esteem issues were born (without this or that thing, I'm not good enough). These were our formative years, our *con*formative years, our fall, that transitioning period when the self-awareness shifted from the natural, inwardly oriented soul that took on a body, to a body-centered self-image that started carrying

[92] Matthew 23:9

[93] Roeder, Mark. 2013. Unnatural Selection: Why The Greeks Will Inherit the Earth. HarperCollins.

the abstract notion of having a soul.

This fundamental shift in identity, this separation of the self-awareness from the soul, becomes for us the "... *way which seems right to a man, but its end is the way to* [spiritual] *death.*"[94]

The day, the very minute that our physical body entered this worldly harbor, was marked, recorded, and certified as the beginning of our existence. Programmed to associate who and what we are at the body level, the birthday clock began ticking, and our body-centered self, exposed and beholden to the restrictions of Newtonian law, kicked in. Suddenly we had our father's eyes or our mother's hair, and a physical brain treated as a blank tablet to be socialized and filled with the information that would enable us to cope with our strange new reality. We became the star pupil or the dumb kid in the class, the athlete or the nerd, the homecoming queen or the plain Jane. We were evaluated, not on the order of the once-familiar eternal scale of the soul, but on a culturally calibrated scale, subject to time and space, genetics, social performance, I.Q., age, looks, rich or poor, popularity and by all else that transpires between the book ends of the birth and death of our physical body. Perhaps our parents and educators determined that our natural talents and interests had no monetary potential and discouraged their development. You and I have stepped into a world that largely ignores the warning of Emerson:

> "Don't be deceived by dimples and curls. I tell you that babe is a thousand years old."

Our world trades in the currency of dimples and curls, and is largely asleep to the soul. The materialists tell us that God is nothing more than a primordial need, a naturally selected configuration of neurons, evolved in the brain as a genetic response to our need to invent meaning in an otherwise meaningless world. The thousand-year-old babe is thrown out with the bathwater the moment the umbilical cord is severed and we are laid to suckle at our mother's breast.

With the intuitive portal all but closed, the self-awareness merges with the ego and takes on the unintended role as the ruling force in the tiny universe that is the self-image and its

---

[94] Proverbs 14:12

accompanying galaxy of consciousness. Consciously cut off from the soul, the self-image measures its strength, worth, and relevance by the type and quality of external positions and possessions it acquires. This false sense of identity engages the visualizing aspect of the imagination and all other faculties in a life-long quest to draw fulfillment from external sources. The cognitive arms race is game on in earnest.

Law of Attraction/Positive Thinking

Those who discover the correlation between their consciousness and their life's conditions may be drawn to a class of teachings that shift the focus from hard labor to positive mental attitudes as a means of acquiring the things they desire. This affirmative approach based on the *law of attraction*, advocates developing and attracting conditions of healing and prosperity through the practice of positive mental attitudes and the power of positive thinking. This approach is good as far as it goes.

From the Gospel of Matthew, we get the sense that Jesus warned against the practice of laying up earthly treasures where moth and rust consume, and where thieves break in and steal,[95] regardless of the method of acquisition employed. Jesus bluntly distinguishes between God and mammon,[96] leaving little doubt that the worship of one meant the denial of the other. And yet, as I've already pointed out, one of the most beautiful passages of scripture also comes from Matthew's account, with Jesus clearly stating that a genuine understanding of our spiritual heritage naturally translates into a life free of fear and material want; a condition already enjoyed by the birds of the air and the lilies of the field.

> "Therefore do not be anxious, saying, 'What shall we eat?' or 'What shall we drink?' or 'What shall we wear?' For the Gentiles seek all these things; and your heavenly Father knows that you need them all. But seek first his kingdom and his righteousness, and all these things shall be yours as well."[97]

We may declare our main interest is in spiritual matters, but we would probably be most honest admitting our motive in seeking

---

[95] Matthew 6:19
[96] Matthew 6:24
[97] Matthew 6:31-33

first the kingdom is simply a means to the greater end of having *all these things*. We are still shackled with the problem of the soul engaged in the human experience from within a physical body whose needs provide much of the incentive that drives our quest for spiritual understanding. We sit up and take notice when a man like Jesus suggests the triumph of spirit over matter. The quest for spiritual understanding can easily take a back seat to finding that elusive key to a restriction-free physical body and material environment.

The context of this saying clearly indicates that the "kingdom" is of far greater value than any material benefits it might generate. In addition, gaining an understanding of it does not seem to involve a patient process of consciousness building that will one day bring our evolving soul into alignment with a universe of material abundance. We are led to believe that it is our understanding and trust in the present and accessible spiritual domain, awaiting our recognition that fulfills our material requirements; a state that brings to mind that carefree harmony between soul and body that we enjoyed in the womb.

Not God or Mammon

The appeal of practical Christianity is the hope that the system Jesus taught will make us masters of our bodies and material environment. How to heal the body, generate prosperity, get a better job, or find our soul mate are the things we're hoping to achieve through a deeper understanding of this kingdom. Though these represent practical solutions to the problems of the human experience, our focus only on what we deem practical may also keep us from asking and seeking answers to some deeper, much larger questions.

In some ways, the notion of spiritual progress becomes a set of blinders focused only on how adept we are at material demonstration. Rather than commit to actually entering this higher sphere, we often treat it as a means of drawing from a basket the goods we desire and solutions to the problems that confront us in this earthly endeavor. The point we may miss in our quest for things is that, from our soul's point of view, it has never been a question of God or mammon. God is one presence, one power expressing at all levels. Our needs are met at each level. Are we settling for just the visible aspect of available support, or do we seek an understanding of that unseen Source that sustains the soul? I do not think Jesus is urging his listener away from fulfilling their material needs. I believe he is coaxing them toward an understanding of the fuller spectrum.

Because Jesus makes an issue of the worship of God and mammon, some have concluded that he was advocating material deprivation. The keyword here is *worship*. To worship is to venerate something as an idol. Whether we are idolizing a stone statue, a religious relic, or a pile of money, there is a difference between seeing an object as a source of power, and seeing it as a symbol or a reminder of that deeper reality that is the source of all power. The trap many fall into with the practice of tithing, for example, is that they designate a percentage of their income as God's. The real power of tithing kicks in when we look beyond percentages and realize that 100% of all that we receive and give is God's.

Veneration of the symbol, seeing it as the object of fulfillment, is worshiping mammon. The symbol is an expression, an effect of the deeper reality. When our priority is to experience and understand at this level, then its material counterpart sheds its status as mammon. Who would consider a peaceful walk in the woods, with all the natural beauty that we see, hear, touch, and smell as mammon? Yet the material aspect of the natural world is the visible counterpart of an underlying, supporting reality we do not see. The issue is not the material realm as the cause of our problems, but our belief that material things can deliver what only the soul can give.

Take No Thought

Jesus' statement that we take no thought, or refrain from being anxious concerning what we shall eat, drink, or wear[98] suggests a method of manifestation that does not require our physical blood, sweat, and tears. It does not tap our subconscious storehouse of information, or engage in the kind of extensive intellectual analysis that normally accompanies our attention to meeting the body's needs. Given its natural means of expression, the soul projects directly from its own self-sustaining existence those ideas necessary to form the consciousness that inspires the kind of physical action that translates into the various aspects of our material environment.

---

[98] Matthew 6:31

In other words, Jesus is suggesting a manifestation process that bypasses altogether all the wants and needs of the self-image we have created. Rather than the self-image, with its fears, inadequacies, and limitations calling the consciousness-building shots, it is from the soul that our flow of instruction comes.

The self-image has hijacked this otherwise very natural flow that we see in play everywhere in nature. Plants and animals do not have the intellectual capacity or the imagination that allows them to establish a self-image capable of interfering with the manifestation process. The soul of the simplest seed is complete. From this soul, a totally fulfilling manifestation process occurs. Why would we, of far greater creative capacity, think of ourselves as being any less equipped than even the least of these?

From this understanding, it is clear that Jesus knew exactly what he was talking about when he urged his listeners to seek first the kingdom and all else would be added. The problem that our self-image encounters with this instruction is that it has subconscious files filled with information on what it believes the "kingdom" is supposed to look like. When it gets no satisfactory results running to these files, it continues its pursuit to understand by checking the files of others. Perhaps if Jesus had not used the term "kingdom" and instead said the answers we seek are encoded in our soul, many might have been saved much grief searching for something in their own memory banks that already exists within their being.

As we begin to reopen the intuitive aspect of the imagination, our soul's light gradually reaches the visioning aspect. New and spontaneous imagery is generated, possibly as mental pictures, but more likely as a deep and secure inner knowing that something transcending our normal thinking is beginning to emerge. This knowing will often come in flashes of insight at unexpected times throughout the day. We recognize the spiritual authenticity of this rising light as a stark contrast to any notion of spiritual illumination our self-image has conjured up thus far.

Our real adventure of contemplation, exploration and discovery on this earth truly begins with the conscious recovery of a soul-based perspective. To use another bit of wisdom attributed to Jesus, though we are missing one of our one hundred sheep, we still own them all.[99] The missing one is the understanding that our

---

[99] Matthew 18:12

soul is now whole. This is but a perceptual problem, a forgetting that we are here in this earthly harbor by choice and we are still fully supplied and supported within the womb of God.

The practice of meditation, which we will explore in the following chapter, has but one purpose. This purpose is to open the intuitive portal of the imagination, to get a firm grasp on our true home at sea, to stir in us the courage to cast off the lines that bind us to this shore, and set sail for the open water

.

CHAPTER 10

MEDITATION

"We stand before the secret of the world, there where Being passes into Appearance, and Unity into Variety" – *Ralph Waldo Emerson, The Poet.*

While meditation may or may not change what we see, it will always change the way we see it. — JDB

The Sanctuary of the Soul

A sanctuary is a consecrated place where one finds refuge from the slings and arrows of the world, but we do not want to think of the sanctuary of the soul as a place to hide. This is our place of reconnecting and aligning our minds with our true Source. Because this connection is subjective, many think of it as secondary in importance to the development of the objective, intellectual aspect of the mind. Conscious connection with your soul is a very real and empowering experience that will do more than anything to enhance the quality of your life. You not only become an observer of the Creative Life Force rising as your soul, you come to know your authentic essence is doing the rising. As a participant, you no longer wonder what the expansive intention of this individualizing process is; you experience it first-hand. This direct knowledge profoundly influences the way you think of yourself, and it will alter the value you place on all things. You become a student of the greatest teacher you could possibly encounter—your own soul.

Do a web search on "meditation images" and you'll find the practice overwhelmingly portrayed as highly elastic young models in designer tights, sitting in the lotus position, fingers held a certain way, the yellow tint of sunlight from that photographically magic moment of the day perfectly highlighting the Buddha like serenity that adorns their young faces. You will be far better off shunning such images, New Age commercialism, and approaching meditation as your own unique discovery. Ultimately it will be your discovery, your process, for as you venture into the experience of your soul, you will find for yourself what works and what does not. You will learn the difference between that "still small voice" and the ceaseless chatter generated by that spiritual wannabe that is your self-image.

God is individualizing as your soul. Think about this. It is as if you own a stretch of beach, and the ocean is, at this very moment, washing your shore. This is your experience. This is your relationship. It is happening in you now, and you have the full capacity to know firsthand who and what you are, and what you intend to do with your current incarnation. In truth, you are the only one who can know this.

We have all fallen into the trap of thinking others are better qualified than we to instruct us on the nature of our own soul. But, this is only because we have not accepted ownership of our unique piece of this beach. This is probably due to the fact that so much has been written on the topic of spirituality. The authorities are those who have retired to a cave in the desert, the cloistered monk, or the Indian guru that can meditate for days on end. In the capitalistically leaning West, we hail as experts the best-selling authors, or the popular talk show hosts who amass a fortune spotlighting them. We are truly undermining our natural, intuitive way of knowing by taking the objective approach to a subjective experience. We are attempting to evolve our spiritual understanding by amassing the catchy clichés from the peddlers of spirituality. Our spiritual understanding is not ours. We are visiting the beach of another. We cannot get to our own beach from here.

Jesus referred to the lilies of the field and the birds of the air as prime examples of the prospering life. These do not reach out away from themselves for the knowledge to successfully interface with their environment. Nor do they stockpile that which, for them, is the wealth that will comfortably sustain their future existence. Every plant and every creature is naturally attuned to the preservation of the body. They do not possess the creative imagination that allows them to invent a false sense of self, or to consider that which sustains it as the epitome of prosperity. Prosperity is that sustaining element embedded in each moment. They flourish in their world, build their homes, reproduce, and feed their families by being true to what they are right now. The robin does not need to soar like the eagle, and the eagle does not pluck worms from the earth.

In our confusion over the reconciliation between the spiritual and material aspects of our experience, we ask others to resolve the questions we have. Their answers become our answers, largely because we admire them, respect their authority, and we want to have an understanding that is similar to theirs. We will never get satisfactory answers until we sit at our own beach and have our own experience. Answers concerning our soul can come only from our own soul. They may be the same answers we receive from another, but we will not embrace them because they *seem* to be true. We embrace them because we *know* they are true.

Form Follows Function

In this book I am taking a broader approach to the practice of meditation than I have in the past. Because all of us have undoubtedly filled our conscious and subconscious files full of information about the various approaches to meditation, our actual attempts at becoming still may end up looking like little more than a search on our computer's hard drive for an abstract notion that we consider an experience with God.

Our field of awareness is an interactive dynamic of consciousness that is very useful to understand, especially as it relates to meditation. There are three types of input that impact our awareness. The two most prominent are our five senses and our memory. The third input source, our intuition, involves feeling at the spiritual level. This input is the most difficult to describe because it is not the same as the intuitive "hunch" many have experienced.

Imagine all three of these input levels have volume knobs. Typically, the senses and memory inputs are set at a much higher volume than the intuitive input. For meditation, we turn down the senses input by finding a quiet place, relaxing the body, and closing our eyes. The memory input continues at full volume, which is why we find our awareness suddenly crowded with everything from appointments to things we're going to say to our co-worker to win that ongoing argument. Senses playback is turned down but memory playback is now more pronounced, like the grandfather clock that ticks away unnoticed through the day but sounds like a blacksmith hammering red hot horseshoes in the still of night.

Our intuitive input channel is not audio/visual but feeling accompanied by direct knowing at the spiritual level. The intuition opens us to an experience of the energy that animates our being. This is as different as the audio/visual function of your computer and the computers electrical connection. Though the electrical connection is the least apparent to you the user, the computer will not function without it.

To illustrate this intuitive aspect, imagine yourself outside at night with a flashlight. You can point the flashlight's beam in any direction you choose. Everything within that beam is within the scope of your awareness. Now imagine the sky is full of stars but, because your flashlight is so bright, the light drowns out much of what you can see in the sky and in your immediate surroundings. You turn off your light and for a few moments you are engulfed in darkness. Then, as your vision gradually adjusts, you begin to experience a sky ablaze with stars, and you can see much more in your immediate surroundings. Your awareness expands from the focal point of your flashlight beam to the grander scale of the night sky. If you were hiking at night through treacherous terrain, it would probably not be wise to try to pick your way through the darkness without the aid of the flashlight. Turning off the light is most useful if you want to enjoy the stars. This broader feeling of context inspires in you the sense that you are part of something vast.

Now suppose you are tent camping, you've hiked away from your camp, and night comes with only the sliver of a moon. You have your flashlight but your camp is too far away to see. You turn your light off and allow your eyes to adjust to the dark. Across the meadow you can see your tent. Knowing your camp's direction, you then turn on your flashlight and make your way back to your camp.

This describes the relationship between meditation and prayer. Meditation is the act of turning off the flashlight so you may get a larger perspective. Prayer is turning on the flashlight so you can find your way to a given point you experienced in meditation. Our intellectually oriented awareness is like the flashlight beam. We use it to focus on this and that thing believing that only those things we see within the scope of our beam represents reality. Yet we know there is much more beyond the beam.

We can think of meditation as the practice of turning off the flashlight, letting our spiritual eyes adjust, and becoming aware of the universe that exists beyond our intellectual beam. With the flashlight on, our awareness is concentrated within the beam. When we turn the light off, we open our mind to a broader field that includes our spiritual environment. Whether our flashlight is on or off, our field of awareness is equally acute.

With this in mind, I suggest rather than thinking of meditation as the single act of stilling the mind and experiencing God, we begin to think of it as a combination of actions and attitudes geared toward increasing awareness of the soul, even with the flashlight on. We find the best ways to lower the volume inputs of the senses and memory, and raise the volume of intuition.

From this perspective, the architectural concept of form following function may serve well. When we understand that the function of every spiritual practice is simply the act of realigning our self-awareness with the soul, then our meditation practice takes a form that best addresses our understanding of this function. Most importantly, the practices become *our* forms rather than those passed on to us from other people. If you are struggling with meditation, it may be that it has a foreign element. You are trying to apply someone else's description of both the problem and the solution. When you look at a problem that you know is within your reach to solve, and you grasp the value of solving it, you will find a solution.

I want to make two suggestions that I think will assist you in your approach to meditation. First, as best you can, refrain from thinking of meditation as an attempt to experience God. Think of it instead as a process of moving your awareness from your self-image to your soul. God, for many, is an abstraction that is too daunting to reach. Experiencing your own soul, on the other hand, is closer to home, a more intimate and accessible objective.

Secondly, if the conditions of your life are not to your liking, do not attempt to use meditation to change them. Doing so is a common mistake that nearly always leads to frustration and discouragement. The changes you will likely see first in your meditation practice will be in your attitudes about your circumstances. As restrictive and out of control as they may feel at the moment, you will begin to see that your circumstances do not have the power to hamper the freeing radiance of your soul. Any impatience you feel concerning your circumstances is your self-image issuing orders on what you should do and what should happen to make it happy. In a moment I'll present a simple technique that will help you turn down the volume of this little dictator. Just be aware that your inner longing for changed circumstances is coming from your self-image rather than your soul. The soul is always content regardless of circumstances.

Your soul is now and has always been instructing you on how to return to it. The spiritual homesickness you feel is your soul calling you home. It is also important to understand that you are responding to this call. Your dissatisfaction with your current state of affairs, in particular, with that information you were given concerning spiritual matters, can and should be taken as an indicator that something in you already inhabits the home you long for. This something, of course, is your soul.

Most of us will interpret our dissatisfaction and spiritual restlessness as some form of lack that is ours to fill. Like the prodigal son who worked out the scheme of returning home as a servant in his father's household, we begin devising the conditions that we believe are necessary for our successful return. Though this son questioned his worthiness, he also reasoned that life as a servant would be better than the life he was living in the foreign land.

Among other things, this parable illustrates that our return home requires no such compromise, no bargaining. It is completely unconditional. I will state again that there are no natural barriers of time and space between where our self-awareness may be now and the rightful home we are seeking. There are some unnatural barriers, and one of the greatest is the belief that spiritual ignorance and soul immaturity are conditions that must be overcome before we can return home. Again, this false belief is generated by the time and space oriented self-image. The prodigal obviously believed his riotous living had compromised his right to return home at any level of heir privilege. It had not dawned on him that the rain still fell and the sun rose just as surely[100] through his moments of starvation as they had when he lived his relatively care free life at home.

We've seen that when we are learning a new skill, time and space factor in. We train our intellect and our muscles to perform in a new way. Intuitive knowing is completely different. To reverse our earlier analogy, it is more like stepping from a dark room into the full light of day. You may have to allow your eyes to adjust to the brightness, but there is nothing you have to learn about the nature of sunlight or how to experience it.

Why Omnipresence Matters

If you look at a photo of the earth taken from space, you see our marbled globe suspended in a sea of black. It appears that there is no light in the blackness, yet the earth, reflecting this otherwise invisible light, is proof that light literally fills the blackness. Think of the omnipresence of God in the same way. The reason it seems that God is not present is because we are looking for God from the shadowed side of the earth. We have invented an idea of what God should look like, and we are looking for something that aligns with this idea.

You know if you are on the dark side of the earth and you simply wait, the earth will turn and you will see the light of day. You also know that there are no learning requirements for this to happen. Time and space factor in because we're talking about earth, sunlight, and the location of your body on earth. It takes the earth a certain amount of time to rotate and expose your position to the sun. As I pointed out in an earlier chapter, if you were able to leave your body and move out of the earth's shadow, you would see the sun shines perpetually.

This is what you are seeking in meditation. You are turning your self-awareness from the intellectually-based senses input to the intuitive way of knowing. As a simple illustration, place your hand in a light source, a lamp with your palm facing the light. The back of your hand will be shadowed. Now turn your hand over so the back is facing the light and your palm is in the shadow. Your palm

---

[100] Matthew 5:45

is like your intellect and the back of your hand your intuition. With this simple demonstration, you see the only thing that changes is which side of your hand you have facing the light. You can turn your hand at will.

To bring this example into the meditative experience, think of your soul rather than God as the perpetual light source. This will help you put aside the idea that something in you needs to be developed before you can experience your spirituality. In terms of its composition, your soul has equal standing with God. Remember, "In the beginning was the Word (soul), and the Word was with God, and the Word was God." Everything is already in place and waiting. Meditation is the act of turning your self-awareness from the shadows to the light that is shining in full force in you, as your soul.

Jesus did not have access to a photo of earth from space but he did use a metaphor that carries the same idea:

> "The wind blows where it wills, and you hear the sound of it, but you do not know whence it comes or whither it goes; so it is with every one who is born of the Spirit."[101]

The wind, like light filling the blackness of space, is unseen. But you do hear it so you know it is present.

The idea we want to take from this is that God, the Creative Life Force behind all manifestation, has individualized as your soul for the purpose of continued expression. This is not a process you and I have started. Nor is it one we can stop. We can come to know this process in a way that gives our soul unhindered, free reign in establishing a spiritually inspired consciousness. The ideas we hold are true of the soul. This inspiration is the *"breath of the Almighty."*[102] When the intellectually based self-image steps in and takes over consciousness building, we become *"man, whose breath is in his nostrils."*[103]

---

[101] John 3:8
[102] Job 33:4, KJV
[103] Isaiah 2:22, KJV

Self Denial

> Then Jesus told his disciples, "If any man would come after me, let him deny himself and take up his cross and follow me."[104]

This saying may carry an air of austerity, but it truly is our key to freedom and prosperity. Self denial is not about letting go of all the things you think you want; it is about letting go of the self that wants them. When, through conscious and deliberate exposure to your soul, you begin to loosen your grip on the false sense of self, your soul fills that vacancy. Your wants are transformed in ways that are compatible with who and what you are at this deepest level. In short, your life begins to work because you are building on the rock of the soul.

The practice of meditation is not an end in itself. It is a means to the end of entering direct communion with your soul. When this communion begins to take place, you are instructed in deeper communion by the experience itself. As your soul reveals more of itself, you lose all sense of burden concerning your quiet time. It's similar to the difference of being forced to study a textbook to pass an exam or reading a good novel that is hard to put down. If you're taking the textbook approach to meditation, try to loosen your attitude about it and make it more user-friendly. Make it your practice of communion with your soul.

The Importance of Context

Whether or not you believe it is true, I hope you are at least beginning to entertain the idea that your soul is complete right now, and that you are getting the sense that you have, for reasons of your choosing, taken on this body. Even the act of considering such things is actually a lite version of meditation that, for a short time, lifts you from the confines of the self-image, and sparks new ways of seeing yourself. You are still on the outside looking in, for simply thinking about your soul does not anchor you in the deeper experience you seek, but it's a beginning. The moment you open your mind to your spiritual possibilities, you are opening the intuitive portal to your soul.

---

[104] Matthew 16:24

I would not recommend using the practice of meditation to try to discover why you incarnated at this time and place. If you've ever had the experience of going into a room for something and then forgetting what you went for, you know the harder you try to remember the more you seem to forget. You usually remember when you stop trying. Free your soul of all preconceived conditions and give it time to emerge in its own way into the field of your awareness. This specific information may naturally reveal itself to you, which is fine if it happens. You want to make your mind an open vessel to your soul by releasing all preconceptions of what may come.

More important than knowing why you took on a body is simply accepting that you could and did do it. Entertaining the idea that you are here by choice, not chance, is a powerful position to be in. More powerful still is the realization that your choice is not permanent. The time will come when you will lay down this body and return to your natural, unencumbered spiritual state. There is much more to you than this sphere of experience into which you have placed your body.

As I stated earlier, I think it is highly likely that we knew there would be maintenance issues and limitations with the body. You and I were willing to experience these because we understood that the times we have spent in bodies, probably many, are relatively brief. Considering the all-knowing aspect of the soul, it would seem incredible not to know this. Even now, we know each of our daily circumstances has a beginning and an end. When we go on a vacation, we know we'll return home. We sit down with a good book knowing we'll reach that final page. And who hasn't had the experience of mulling over a span of decades, wondering where the time went?

It is when we are suffering that it seems our struggle will never end. Prolonged suffering can push some into such a self-absorbed state that the world created by the self-image totally implodes and a complete breakdown, even suicide, appears to be the only way out. While exploring this subject is beyond the scope of this book, reasons for reaching such a depressed state are commonly derived from attempts to fit into a role that runs counter to the soul's true nature. The self-image falsely believes it cannot go on without certain conditions or relationships in place. In truth, nothing in the self-image's collapsing world is required by the soul. The soul is our true, God-sustained center of power. Your soul's wholeness, its strength and purpose, is not dependent on people, places, and things. The shift in awareness from self-image to this authentic dimension through meditation brings the deeply healing spiritual element that truly is greater than anything in the world cobbled together by the surface self.

Meditation clears the film from our spiritual vision and brings the eternal perspective into the field of our awareness in ways that will likely be different from anything we expect. This awareness rises as very gentle, nearly imperceptible energy that is quite natural though rarely experienced in the endless humdrum of the mind's senses-based traffic. As your inner vision is raised, much will come to mind that will guide you in putting the pieces of your life's puzzle together. Your desire to experience more of this energy is the guiding direction. It will not prompt you with words, but with its very essence. You will learn through direct experience how to position your mind in ever deepening receptivity.

Our purpose with meditation is not to ignore the body, but to transcend its influence long enough to reacquaint ourselves with the soul that actually animates it. In the following chapter, we'll explore a variety of techniques ranging from simple exercises in perceptual awareness to those that can help you move deeper into a first-hand experience with the completeness of your soul.

CHAPTER 11

MEDITATION EXERCISES

The meditation exercises that follow represent such a wide range of commitment that everyone can do at least one. I'm suggesting a variety of options because most people I talk to about meditation struggle with it. There is much confusion about how we are to think, relax, position our bodies, and, most difficult of all, how we're supposed to focus on something as abstract as communion with God, or even the soul. The subjective nature of the meditative experience makes it difficult to describe objectively. We normally think of relaxation as the mind and body at rest, but the meditative posture is a mind on full alert. Choosing quality time when we are not likely to drift into sleep is important.

As we've seen in the previous chapter, think of meditation as turning off the flashlight, and letting your spiritual eyes adjust to the universe that exists beyond that intellectual beam. With the flashlight on, your awareness is concentrated within the beam. When the light is off, you adjust to the broader field of your spiritual environment. Whether your flashlight is on or off, your field of awareness is equally acute. When you turn off your flashlight, you don't fall asleep. You transition from using your daylight vision to night vision. Instead of analyzing everything in the flashlight beam—rock, tree stump, bush—you simply let the darkness happen. You are no less aware, not the least bit drowsy, but you see in a different way. Your eyes and all of your senses adjust to the night. You have done this countless times without giving it much thought. You have also had the reverse experience of being in darkness and having someone turn on a light. The light blinded you briefly, but your eyes adjusted. In both cases, your vision adapted to the change in your environment. You do not associate drowsiness with either situation.

This is the point of meditation. You are placing yourself in a condition that is receptive to the experience of your soul, that spiritual dimension within you that is accessed through the intuitive portal. In one sense, this faculty has rarely been used in the way you will use it in meditation. The flashlight of the intellect has shown so brightly that when you attempt to turn it off through relaxation, nothing seems to happen. Your *night vision*, that is, your spiritual vision has not engaged, at least not in the way you are expecting. Learn to give it the needed time to do so.

Observing how your night vision gradually engages is a simple exercise worth performing.

Exercise #1: Observing Your Night Vision

For this very simple exercise, you will need a flashlight. With the flashlight in hand and turned off, enter a room that is fully lighted, and then turn off the lights. Observe how poor your vision is but how it gradually adjusts to the dark. As your vision naturally adjusts, you're not required to do anything but wait. There is no need to strain to see through the darkness. You also notice that the darkness does not bring drowsiness. Your mind is alert and observing. Your body knows how to make the necessary adjustments to this change in your environment. The longer you wait, the better you see.

Once your eyes have fully adjusted to the dark, turn on your flashlight and scan the room for a few moments, taking in all you see. Now turn off the flashlight and see what has happened to your vision. You will notice two things are going on. You have again lost much of your night vision and, you are probably remembering the images in the room while your flashlight was on.

What you can learn from this exercise

In the context of meditation, relaxation is the process of letting go of your normal, light-oriented way of seeing and allowing your night vision to emerge. Once your eyes have adjusted to the dark, you can see most objects in the room. But seeing objects in the room is not your objective. Your objective is to allow your night vision to establish itself. If your objective is to see the things in the room, you do something very different. You turn on the light.

When you try to still your mind and yet find yourself thinking about events in your life, this is like turning on your flashlight and scanning the room. Relaxation, then, is letting go of your normal vision and allowing your intuitive vision to emerge. Given the chance, your intuitive vision knows how to do this, no learning required. In fact, there is something you must *stop* doing. You must stop scanning the objects, all the various situations that make up your life. You relax this mental *seeing* and turn your intuitive receptivity to the natural radiance of your soul, which we'll explore in the exercise, *A Full Meditation*.

What I want to make clear with this exercise is that the process we call meditation is as natural as the process of gaining night vision. In all likelihood, the only obstacle you are dealing with is that of making meditation a foreign practice. You are seeking an experience of your soul with the flashlight of your intellect, that visualizing aspect of your imagination. Relax this effort knowing your intuitive portal, like your eyes adjusting to the dark, knows how to adjust to the subtle radiance of your soul.

Exercise #2: Practice Seeing

Here is another exercise that demonstrates that you can see a thing inaccessible to your normal vision. This exercise utilizes a *stereogram*. If you're not familiar with stereograms, perform an Internet search for the term and you'll find a variety of examples.

When you look at the stereogram with your normal vision, you will see a multi-colored, two-dimensional graphic consisting of patterns that make little sense. Allow your eyes to relax and a three-dimensional object will *magically* appear. You may see a fish, a human figure, a flower or any other object the artist embedded. If you look at the stereogram in your normal viewing mode, and someone tells you there's a dolphin in the picture, you'll look for the dolphin hidden in the patterns, which you won't find. The harder you try, the more it will evade you.

The secret behind seeing the three-dimensional object in that maze of patterns is to turn off your object-seeking flashlight, so to speak. This, of course, seems counter-intuitive. Normally, if someone points out an object in the distance that you do not see, you'll double your effort to sharpen your focus, which will probably work. You are also using this type of seeing as you read the words on this page. If you view these printed words in the same way you look at a stereogram, however, you will see double, making the text very difficult to read. In daily life, we don't have much use for this way of seeing so we seldom use it. Daydreaming might be the closest. We find ourselves staring at nothing in particular because we're watching some mental scene play out.

Like blurred vision, we don't have much practical use for the kind of intuitive perception we're talking about, which is why we have reduced our understanding of this faculty to those occasional hunches, premonitions, or gut feelings. I'll say again that the practice of meditation is not about cultivating extra sensory perception, that the intuition is *not a sixth sense* but a faculty designed specifically for experiencing the soul and bringing its influence into our field of awareness. As you open to this experience, intuition begins to play a significant role in your daily decision-making, becoming a major influence on the way you employ all other executive faculties.

Exercise #3: Simple Contemplation

Your initial approach to meditation may be the simple contemplation throughout your day of the idea that your soul is now complete and fully accessible; that the restlessness you feel is your soul calling you home. In reading up to this point, you have already started this contemplative activity. This does not fit the meditation model of sitting still, eyes closed, attention turned away from senses input and seeking an inner experience, but it is a move in the right direction.

For a number of reasons, people who take a full-scale approach to meditation often do so without success. If you are among those who have not experienced the deeper levels of your being through meditation, doing more of the same will not produce different results. A key reason for your lack of success may be as simple as trying to apply ideas and practices that are foreign to you. You want to find your own, user-friendly approach that will produce gratifying results.

As we have seen, the problem we face with meditation is that our self-awareness is focused more on the self-image than on the soul. Because this has been our status quo for most of our life, we will do better gently inviting the soul into our field of awareness. We can't force this to happen, mainly because we don't know how. We can learn to let it happen by dwelling on the truth that our soul already knows how to enter our field of awareness. Most of us, thinking books and teachers hold the key to our success, have looked with great hope to these external sources for help, when our true help is already at hand. Who could possibly sit where you sit, at the very center of your self-awareness, and view your life and all its many issues from the unique perspective that you hold? Who knows you better than you? If you make a shift in your thinking and approach your soul experience as if it is your problem and only you can find the solution, you put yourself in the proper frame of mind that brings your awakening. You want to call on an expert, but until you are willing to make yourself that expert, your results will not be satisfying.

Exercise #4: A Walking Meditation

This walking meditation requires the least amount of concentration. I'm calling it a walking meditation because it is one you can practice in any normal routine throughout your day. This meditation consists of a simple visualization and two affirmations.

Visualization: Hold at your core the vision of a dazzling light radiating through your entire being. Think of your intuitive portal as completely open so the light of your soul shines into your conscious mind, your body, and out into your surroundings.

With this visualization, use the following two affirmations:

My soul is complete.

The light of my soul is shining in its full power right now.

You can practice this visualization and the two affirmations right now. Don't be too concerned about whether or not you are doing it exactly in the right way. You are instilling the awareness that your soul is present and shining forth in its full capacity now, and you are bringing this awareness into your normal routine.

I'm calling this a walking meditation, but you may practice it during a telephone conversation, while shopping, while in a board meeting, or while working in your garden. In other words, you practice it anytime during the normal activities of your day.

To understand the objective of this simple exercise, let's first take a look at two things you are not trying to achieve with it. You are not seeking to reprogram your subconscious mind by establishing a new habit, and you are not attempting to experience full-blown cosmic consciousness.

Concerning the first point, a habit is an automatic pattern of behavior. Meditation, at any level, is mindfulness, experiential in nature, not a practice that runs on subconscious autopilot.

To the second point, a breakthrough in awareness can occur at any moment and will, more often than not, happen when you're not expecting it. The walking meditation will certainly open you to deeper experiences, but the moment you make these your objective, your self-image will take over and begin manufacturing experiences. Relieve yourself of this pressure.

What you are doing with this simple exercise is initiating the move of your self-awareness from your self-image to your soul. Your subconscious mind will respond in its own way to any change of consciousness "chemistry" that takes place. Also, bear in mind that your longing to have a cosmic experience has its origin in the self-image. Your soul has never known anything but cosmic consciousness.

The walking meditation, like all forms of meditation, is based on the law of expression. You are initiating a cause—bringing your soul to your awareness—and you are taking your mind off all potential effects that this might have. Your soul has a very different agenda than your self-image and it informs you of this agenda intuitively, through inspiration.

A walk by yourself, in a park or some natural setting if possible, is a good time to practice your walking meditation. Start out walking normally. After a time, stop, close your eyes, take a few relaxing breaths, and then begin to see light radiating from the core of your being. It's okay that this is just a mental picture. You don't want to try to force anything else to happen. Make the statement, *My soul is complete.* A few moments later, still holding your vision, say, *The light of my soul is shining in its full power right now.* Get some sense that this is true and begin walking, slowly and deliberately. Repeat both affirmations as you walk while holding the vision. Continue this for as long as it feels productive.

You can practice the walking meditation during any activity, even those where other people are involved. With practice you will be able to run it in the background of your mind even when you are in conversation with other people. I often do it when I am delivering a Sunday morning talk or even teaching a class. It always brings a transcendent element to my thought that has freed me from the need to use notes. You will find your own best, most effective way to employ this meditation technique. You may change the affirmations and expand on the visualization, but keep it simple, and keep it focused.

Exercise #5: Bagging the Self-Image

A productive meditation practice is one that lays aside all preconceived forms of meditation and focuses instead on the function of moving your self-awareness from your senses-based self-image to your soul. Understanding this function, you will find your own form for getting there. To do this, you want to experience the soul at some level. If you do not have a measure of experience with your soul, you will not know where you are going with any meditative practice. Even the slightest experience with the soul gives you something to build on, a true direction to follow.

Let's take a look at a couple is exercises that can be a helpful catalyst for the experience of the soul.

Imagine you have a large canvas bag. In this bag you place your self-image with all of its childhood memories, its spiritual aspirations, its dark secrets, its talents and skills, its body-centered identity, its confusion, its family ties, its career, its successes and failures, its fears, its hopes and dreams. Nothing you put in this bag is you. This is your self-image and its history. The real you, your soul, is the observer of this bag and its contents.

With this picture clearly in mind, allow yourself to experience this freeing realization:

> I am here right now. I am an eternal soul grounded in and sustained by the life, love, power and intelligence of God. I have consciousness. I can think and I can feel, and I have a physical body that enables me to communicate with other people and to interact with all aspects of my material environment.

I am not the contents of this bag. I am under no obligation to re-open it and take on all of its problems. I am *not* this. I am me. I am my soul, free to use my consciousness and my body to experience earth in any manner of my choosing.

As you hold this simple image, you will feel as if a great weight is being lifted from your being. Stress literally drains from your body. Your mind rests in the peace of the simplicity of being.

Everything you think you know about meditation is in this bag. Let it go. The experience you are having now, the freedom and peace of letting go, is the direction your meditation will take from this moment on. Stop pursuing the experience of foreign gods and realize that you already are what you are looking for.

Exercise #6: Guided Meditation

To experience it, you first direct your faith to the truth that your soul is present, fully accessible and absolutely familiar. Take the attitude that you are not traveling into a far country but that you are coming home.

Let's expand on Exercise #5 with the understanding that this is a guided meditative exercise, a framework whose purpose is to open your intuitive portal to a more spontaneous, self-directed experience. As with any exercise of this type, the imagery is intended to help you achieve a measure of the action it suggests. The visualization of bagging your self-image is intended to identify and invoke the feeling of separation between your soul and this senses-generated aspect of your consciousness. The emergence of the soul into the field of your self-awareness is a natural transition that will ultimately require no visual assistance.

Read the steps first and then go back and perform each one. If at any time you find yourself tensing up by trying to force things to happen, let go and relax again.

Step 1: As in the previous exercise, mentally place your self-image and all its problems and concerns into your canvas bag. Cinch it and set it aside.

Step 2: As you observe this bag for a moment, feel yourself relax and become free from the self-image and all of its many issues. If at any time during this exercise you become distracted, remind yourself that you have placed your self image in this bag and you are under no obligation to give it your attention.

Step 3: As you observe the bag and its contents, realize that you are making this observation from the outermost region of your soul, a position that is least in the kingdom.[105] You acknowledge that your bagged self-image is one thing and you, the observer, are something different.

Step 4: Leave your bag and its contents and begin to move to your inner depths, into your soul's sanctuary through the intuitive portal that your faith has now opened. Here you find a dazzling galaxy of energy, absolutely peaceful, all-accepting and totally freeing. You feel very natural and alive.

Step 5: Now move to the center of this energy and experience yourself as its actual source. This pure energy that you are radiates from your core, through the walls of your inner sanctum, engulfs your entire body, and moves out in all directions beyond the farthest reaches of your vision.

Step 6: From your radiant center, speak the words, *I Am*, slowly and several times, each time letting go and allowing your experience to deepen.

Stay with this until you feel ready to get up and go about your day.

Exercise #7: Self-Guided Meditation

This exercise uses your own recorded voice. If you do not have one, there are many inexpensive voice recorders available. If you are not used to hearing your voice on a recording, you may resist this practice. Most people do not think they sound like themselves but if you play your voice to any of your family and friends, they will identify it as yours immediately. Make peace with your voice, because using it can add power to your self-guided meditation.

You may find it adds a soothing aspect to your recording if you play some good meditation music as you make your recording. We'll base this Self-Guided Meditation on the full meditation you will find in Exercise #8.

---

[105] Matthew 11:11

117

Recording Tips

Prior to making this recording, familiarize yourself with your voice recorder. Most recording devices are very simple to use. Do a couple of practice runs by reading a few passages from this book. The recorder will have a built-in microphone, so be sure to hold it steady. Moving it in your hand will generate unwanted noise. Hold the microphone about four to five inches from your mouth. Keep the microphone positioned to one side of your mouth rather than speaking directly into it. This will help you avoid getting the *pop* of your p's.

If you decide to use background music, do a few practice runs. Start the music on whatever device you will use, record your voice with the music playing then check your levels. You do not want the music to overpower your voice. In addition to music, there are also pre-recorded nature sounds available that you may prefer. Some like the sounds of a gentle rain, the surf, or other combinations of natural sounds. Do a search for *soothing sounds* on Youtube.com and you'll find numerous choices.

Each of us has a reading voice and we have a speaking voice. You will be reading passages, but practice using the same speaking voice you would if you were offering comforting words to a child. Without being overly dramatic, let your voice be natural and full of compassion. Speak from your soul. If you feel intimidated by the recorder, work with it until you move past this discomfort. The only audience you are speaking to is yourself. If you make your recording and decide it doesn't feel natural as you listen to it, re-do it until you are satisfied. You will get the best quality of playback sound by listening through an inexpensive pair of ear buds.

The words **Speak** and **Pause** will precede each instruction. Do not speak any of the words in bold print. The ellipsis within sentences indicate a pause of roughly five or ten seconds. The word **Pause** represents a roughly thirty second pause. There is no need to time these, just speak in a relaxed manner.

Making the Recording

Pause: Start the music or your background sounds and let it play for about 30 seconds.

Speak: I close my eyes, relax my body and I let go of all concerns. … I bring my attention to the center of my being. …   My soul is at peace.

Pause

Speak: I dedicate myself to this quiet time by releasing all mental and emotional strife. ... I continue to relax and let go.

Pause

Speak: My soul radiates the pure light and life of God. ... The light of my soul shines warmly and gently into the field of my awareness. ... I do not search for my soul or for my center. ... I am guided to my center by the natural radiance of my soul.

Pause

Speak: I Am. ... As I speak these words, I speak them from my center. ... I Am. ... I Am. ... I am open and receptive to the radiant energy of my soul. ... I Am. ... I Am.

Pause

Speak: The pure energy of life, love, power and intelligence radiates through my entire being. ... There is no need to force anything. ... I let go in perfect trust. ... I let go.

Pause

Speak: My mind is at rest. ... My body is at peace. ... I let go. ... I relax and I let go.

Pause

Speak: I Am. ... I Am. ... My soul is complete, a radiant light that shines from my center. ... The pure radiance of my soul shines in its fullness now. ... I relax and I let this pure energy rise into my awareness.

Pause for about 1 minute

Speak: I Am. ... I Am. ... My mind is at rest. ... My body is at peace. ... I move deeper into relaxation. ... I let go. ... I relax and let go.

Pause

Speak: My soul is complete, a radiant light that shines from my center. ... The pure radiance of my soul shines in its fullness now. ... I relax and I let go.

Pause for one or two minutes and End

Speak: Thank you God. ... Amen

Note: End your meditation with words of your choosing, not necessarily *Amen*. Let the music continue to play for thirty seconds to one minute, bringing the volume down slowly. When the volume is down, turn off the recorder. Prior to using this guided meditation, follow the same preparation you find in Exercise #8, A Full Meditation.

Exercise #8: A Full Meditation

In this full meditation, you will apply no particular techniques or invoke specific elements as you will in exercises #9 through #12. In this full meditation, your objective is to turn down the volumes of the senses and the memory inputs and open your field of awareness specifically and directly to your soul.

A Few Words on Preparation

Preparation for all meditation exercises that follow will be the same as this one. Establish a place within your home where you will not be disturbed. Choose a time when you are most alert. My personal preference is early morning, before I become engaged in the events of the day. Your best time will likely be different. Consistency with quality time rather than a random squeezing into an otherwise busy schedule will factor into your success. Sit in a comfortable chair or on a cushion on the floor with your back supported. Your body is constantly vying for your attention, so you want to minimize the discomfort of poor circulation and other physical distractions.

Begin by relaxing and dedicating yourself to your present purpose by releasing all mental and emotional strife. There will be times when you are unable to let go of a particularly distressing circumstance, so don't try to force it out of your mind. If you cannot release it but find yourself dwelling on it, you will only magnify the problem. It may be best to abandon your attempt at a full meditation for now and come back to it later. The walking meditation might be more suitable at such times.

Close your eyes and let your attention drop to the center of your being. You do not want to make an issue of a physical location, but you will likely find your awareness hovering around the solar plexus, the pit of the stomach. You may realize that you carry stress in this area. If so, acknowledge it and begin releasing it.

Your soul is your center, a natural radiance of energy that will emerge into your increasingly undisturbed field of awareness. You will not need to engage in a search for your center. Just go with what seems right and natural. You may also open your eyes, read a few lines of these instructions to help interrupt and redirect any rising mental chatter.

With your attention at your center, speak the words, *I Am.* Listen and feel from this place. You're not listening for voices and you're not feeling for any preconceived ideas of love or any level of power. You are opening your intuition to the radiant energy of your soul. This radiance is the energy of life, love, power and intelligence but there is no need to focus on any of these. Do not try to force or generate imagery or any kind of experience. You want to get the sense that your soul is a perpetually radiant center at the core of your being. Let yourself go. Allow your thoughts to slow down and let your body continue to release pent up stress. You are not pushing the body away as if any movement or attention to it will crack the silence. Just as your vision will adjust to the darkness when you turn off your light, so your spiritual vision will adjust as you turn down the volume of the senses and that normally active exchange between your consciousness and subconscious mind.

When your mind begins to wander, return your attention to your center and repeat the phrase, *I Am.* Bring your awareness back into the moment and to your purpose for being here. Again, you may open your eyes and adjust your body from time-to-time and then re-center your awareness on the radiance of your soul. When you actually pick up on this radiance, it will not likely be anything visual. It will be a subtle experience of energy that you will discover is always present beneath the threshold of your constant body signaling and the incessant mental chatter. Don't try to do anything with this energy. Just let it move in you as it will. You may wish to acknowledge and enhance the experience by speaking these words softly:

The pure radiance of my soul shines in its fullness now.

I relax and I let this pure energy rise.

Stay with this practice for as long as you can without forcing anything. An aggressive pursuit of inner stillness will not work. But neither will quickly giving in to the constant chatter of your mind. You will make some effort to move past it. Otherwise, your quiet time will yield no experience beyond that of your normal thinking.

There will be times when you are more successful than others so you do not want to measure your progress by how you feel from any given session. It is likely that your first manifestations of this inner reflection will bubble forth during your normal day as an unexpected feeling of gratitude or peace. If you have felt trapped in your life, a new sense of present possibilities may begin to emerge into your awareness. Your circumstances may or may not change, but your appreciation for all aspects of your life can grow in ways that cause you to see things differently. These experiences, as we'll see in the following chapter, will be strengthened, affirmed and enhanced by incorporating them into your consciousness through prayer.

Your goal with meditation is not to change your life. Your goal is to invite your soul into your field of awareness, to know its presence and energy as real. Because this exposure will change the way you see yourself, it will change the way you interact with all the many aspects of your environment. In all likelihood, this new interaction will take you in a direction you would not have otherwise considered, so in thinking of your soul, become willing to forgo all your expectations and let it reveal itself on its own terms.

Focused Meditations

It is sometimes useful to focus specifically on one of your soul's four characteristics as a way of stimulating the energy they represent. The meditation on life, for example, will stir more enthusiasm, which can get you past lethargy. Focusing on love will stimulate deeper understanding in relationships, or various conditions where understanding is called for. If you lack strength—physical strength, strength of character, or strength to carry on some important task—the meditation on power will boost your strength. If you feel the need for more order in your life in general, or in a specific undertaking, the meditation on intelligence will be an appropriate choice.

Like the sun, your soul does not radiate partial frequencies. It gives all of itself all of the time. Your focus on individual aspects will enhance your awareness of that element expressing through you, but you can trust that all four elements are always working in perfect balance with each other.

Exercise #9: Life - Enthusiasm

Follow the same preparations stated above. You are still going to drop your awareness to the area of the solar plexus and center with the phrase, *I Am*. You may also want to use these same statements or some variation for focus.

The pure radiance of my soul shines in its fullness now.

I relax and I let this pure energy rise.

As you relax with your awareness at your center, see the radiating energy of your soul as the energizing life that permeates all aspects of your being. It is natural to visualize life as the light that animates and heals every cell of your body and brings a sparkle of enthusiasm to your eye. You need not direct the energy of life, for life knows how to express itself. We see it expressed in countless ways, forms, and levels everywhere in the world. Life never stagnates. It is only our focus of attention that becomes dull and lifeless. Simply acknowledge the free reign of life as it radiates its natural expansive movement through and as your being. Encourage its flow with words like these:

My soul radiates the pure, unrestricted energy of life.

There are no blockages. There are no restrictions.

I am filled with boundless life and unbridled enthusiasm.

Don't try to pump up your enthusiasm and strive to be the life of the party. Doing this will expend your energy by directing it to that bottomless pit of your unenthusiastic self-image. Any forced positive attitude you generate will be short-lived and costly. A forced expression of enthusiasm is a performance you'll be expected to repeat. People who do this might be entertaining, but they can also be quite wearisome. You don't have to instruct fire to be hot and you don't have to inform life that it needs to express as enthusiasm. Natural enthusiasm manifests as genuine interest in whatever you happen to be doing, from creating a piece of art to taking out the trash. Enthusiasm is as unconditional as the energy of life itself. You need no particular reason to be enthusiastic. It is life's gift to you. As you affirm life in your meditative experience, quiet enthusiasm will naturally grow.

Exercise #10: Love - Understanding

Follow your same meditative preparations and bring your awareness into the region of the solar plexus. See and feel your soul radiating love. This beautiful energy of love works for the highest good of all concerned, sometimes attracting and sometimes repelling or dissolving, depending on how the highest good is to manifest. Whether love attracts or dissolves is not a decision you make, but one you trust love to sort out as it flows in and through every aspect of your being and your life. Love lifts your vision in a way that imparts the understanding to see and know what needs to be done. Affirm:

I am guided by the understanding that love imparts. Love
is my essence. Love is my being. Love is the balancing
action in all my relationships and all conditions in my life.

See your body immersed in love. See every aspect of your life, especially those areas that are troubled, completely engulfed in the love that radiates as your soul. See love doing its perfect work and become willing to do your part in that work when the understanding dictates. Loving your neighbor may result in strengthening your relationship or dissolving it. This is a much better alternative than trying to force yourself to love them because you think you are supposed to. You may not always be able to muster the kind word or take that right action that will bring agreement with another. Still, you can know that invoking love will fit all the pieces together, will tie up the loose ends, and move all concerned to their best and highest good. Love reveals that this is true even when your good intentions at diplomacy fail miserably, or fear drives your own actions. The love that expresses as your soul is greater than all human frailty. Your unloving thoughts and actions or the unloving thoughts and actions of another do nothing to alter love itself. Love does not depend on how loving or unloving you are.

Let all of this go and simply see your entire being immersed in love. Experience love's healing warmth. Let it melt away your stress and your struggle to be loved. You are more than loved. You are love itself.

Exercise #11: Power - Strength

Initiate your normal preparations for meditation. This time you will focus on power. Power manifests in a wide range of ways, from the unfathomable power of the sun to the simple unfolding of a leaf. Power divides our cells and fuels all aspects of our being.

Power rises in your being as physical, mental, emotional, and spiritual strength. You may call on strength to hold a steady course, to take one more step when your world seems to crumble around you, or to steady your faith in the well-being of a loved one. Strength may manifest as the courage to make an apology or it may express as the power to say *no* to behavior you know as destructive.

With your attention focused at the solar plexus, sense the power of your soul rising from your center and radiating throughout your being. Affirm:

I am an expression of pure power. The full radiance of my soul empowers me to steadfastness in all that I am and all that I do. My strength is boundless, my power has no limits.

If you are feeling powerless to do anything about some condition in your life, release the emotional energy of helplessness as you use this affirmation. Again, do not try to make anything happen or even look for changes in your life. Simply allow the flow of power to rise in your being and know it expresses as the strength you need, as you need it. Take a series of deep breaths. With each one, breathe in power and breathe out strength. Power is the essence of your being. You are never without it.

Exercise #12: Intelligence - Order

Prepare yourself for meditation. As your attention drops to the area of your solar plexus, open your mind to the quickening presence of intelligence. Your entire being is already permeated with intelligence. The functions of your body are all governed by it. You see and experience intelligence as order in your breathing, the beating of your heart, and all the many activities within the universe of your body of which you are not even aware. You see intelligence in the flower, in your pet, in the birds, and the clouds that sail across the sky.

As you relax and let go, get the sense of this truth that you are completely immersed in intelligence and that your life is now unfolding in perfect order. Affirm:

> *The very essence of my being is intelligence. My mind is clear. My thinking is orderly. I see things in their highest relation to the whole. My vision is clear. My soul is imbued with the wisdom of the universe. In all I do, I move forward in confidence and in peace.*

Release all feelings of uncertainty about your life and know the intelligence of your soul is guiding your every step. Lift your spiritual eyes away from all appearances and see yourself as a conduit through which infinite intelligence is expressing as you. Everyone and everything becomes part of success in living. If your life seems to be pushing you to the left when you think you should go right, then know the intelligence expressing as your soul is now at work. Do not strain to work out plans or struggle to control events. Hold fast to the truth that the wisdom of your soul is directing your life, that the order and success you desire is unfolding with every new development.

Exercise #13: Simple steps given by Emilie Cady

The following exercise is adapted from Emilie Cady's book, *Lessons In Truth*. For background, read the two chapters from that book, *The Secret Place of the Most High*, and *Finding the Secret Place*.

Withdraw for a time from the outside world. Turn your thoughts within by directing this series of statements to God. Do not speak these statements rapidly, one after another, but dwell on each one, realizing the truth of the words.

You abide within me, You are alive there now.

You are all power.

You are the fulfillment of all I desire.

Your innermost presence now radiates from the center to the circumference of my being.

I give thanks that You hear and answer me, that You now come forth into my visible world as the fulfillment of my desire.

Repeat these statements as needed, not anxiously or with strained effort, not reaching out and up and away to an outside God; but let the words be the quiet, earnest uplifting of the heart to a higher something right within itself, even to "the Presence in me." Let it be made with the quietness and assurance of a child speaking to its loving parent.

Be absolutely still. Relax every part of your being and believe that it is being done.

If you find your mind wandering, bring it right back by going over again the series of statements, speaking them aloud if necessary.

Do not look for signs and wonders, but just be still and know that the very thing you want is flowing in and will come forth into manifestation either at once or a little farther on.

3 conditions:
1. Wait upon God. Do not simply run in and out but dwell in the secret place of the Most High.
2. Let your expectation be from God alone.
3. Do not let waiting in the silence become a bondage to you. If you find yourself getting into a strained attitude of mind or heady, get up and go about some external work for a time. Or, if you find that your mind will wander, do not insist on concentrating; for the moment you get into a rigid mental attitude you shut off all inflow of the Divine into your consciousness.

What to Expect
You will have a strange new consciousness of serenity and quiet, a feeling that something has been done, that some new power to overcome has come to you.

CHAPTER 12

PRAYER

"In what prayers do men allow themselves! That which they call a holy office is not so much as brave and manly. Prayer looks abroad and asks for some foreign addition to come through some foreign virtue, and loses itself in endless mazes of natural and supernatural, and mediatorial and miraculous. Prayer that craves a particular commodity, anything less than all good, is vicious. Prayer is the contemplation of the facts of life from the highest point of view. It is the soliloquy of a beholding and jubilant soul. It is the spirit of God pronouncing his works good. But prayer as a means to effect a private end is meanness and theft. It supposes dualism and not unity in nature and consciousness. As soon as the man is at one with God, he will not beg. He will then see prayer in all action." – *Emerson*

Breaking It Down

It may seem like an unneeded complication to dissect prayer into its various components. Yet prayer engages multiple, commonly and spontaneously used functions of the mind that deserve examination. We can pray one moment, then turn around the next, and use those same functions to worry that our prayer will have no effect. Without some understanding of the role each of these faculties plays, we can easily turn our focus from the joy of a potential solution to mulling over an endless series of negative *what ifs*.

To recap, in this book I am identifying five executive faculties that influence our experience with prayer. These faculties are *imagination, faith, judgment, will,* and *elimination*. We have seen that the imagination has two functions: the *intuitive* and *visualizing* aspects. Meditation opens the intuitive side while prayer focuses on the more intellectual, visualizing feature.

We have discussed how faith can be focused in many directions, some helpful and some not. In prayer, we consciously turn our faith in the direction of our desired good, as if it were an accomplished fact. We see a reference to both faith and imagination in these inspiring words of Jesus:

> "Therefore I tell you, whatever you ask in prayer, believe that you have received it, and it will be yours."[106]

To believe you have received something that you do not already have is to imagine you have it now. This is a combination of *imagination* and *faith*. You employ your best *judgment* in discerning actions and conditions that might be conducive to bringing about this desire. Your faculty of *will* keeps your faith and imagination focused. You employ your faculty of *elimination* by releasing all doubt concerning the bringing forth of your desire.

Again, turning to our flashlight illustration, we can think of meditation as turning off the flashlight and perceiving our larger spiritual context. Prayer would be turning on the flashlight and, with a broader spiritual vision in place, making our way through the terrain of our life. Without the insights provided by the experience of meditation, prayer, as Emerson pointed out, ". . . *looks abroad and asks for some foreign addition to come through some foreign virtue, and loses itself in endless mazes of natural and supernatural, and mediatorial and miraculous.*" In other words, prayer disconnected from the soul, employed to bolster or simply gratify the self-image, is the prayer that craves a particular commodity and is, according to Emerson, *vicious*. I wouldn't necessarily use this strong of a term, but he makes the point.

---

[106] Mark 11:24

One of the keys to understanding prayer in the context we're considering here is found in this statement of Jesus: "... *whatever you ask in prayer* ..." Is the *you* that you are referencing centered in the soul or is it centered in the self-image? Who is doing the asking?

The self-image, operating from a paradigm of separation, always uses prayer to look abroad. Your soul, operating from the paradigm of oneness, employs prayer as a consciousness-building tool. The experiences and knowledge you gain through the meditative process are the starting point for prayer. The spiritual light experienced in our innermost depths needs an outlet. That outlet will take multiple forms in our material world, the best of which are those soul-inspired areas about which we are most passionate.

In using this book, you don't want to say, "Okay, I read the section on meditation and now I want to figure out how to get what I want with prayer." The insights you gain in meditation will dramatically increase your understanding and the effectiveness of your prayer work. Again, as Emerson points out, "*Prayer is the contemplation of the facts of life from the highest point of view.*" Your soul-inspired awareness maintains the highest point of view, synchronizing your external life with the inner promptings of your soul.

One of the first things we need to understand is that even when our minds are scrambling aimlessly from one thought to the next, we are employing every faculty we use in prayer, only we don't call it prayer. It is the white noise of incessant mental chattering. If we think of prayer as the contemplation of facts from the highest point of view, this contemplative process will not include the usual random darting about of our mind.

Our normal approach to prayer is that we spend a few minutes putting in our order and hoping God will fill it while we go about our mental meandering over the endless issues that come packaged with each new hour. We expect God to behave differently by giving us different results while we continue behaving very much the same as we did prior to putting in our order. We may contemplate the facts from the highest point of view for ten minutes then spend the rest of the day contemplating and reacting to the facts from the level of a chaotic self-image. Whether we call it prayer, worry, or simply aimless meandering of thought, we engage exactly the same faculties as we do in prayer. The result is a life shaped less by those few moments dedicated to prayer and more by how we employ our faculties throughout the day.

Imagine a child, amused by the noise he can make, banging away all day long at the keys of a piano. Then, for fifteen minutes, a concert pianist sits down and plays a most beautiful and soothing piece. When she leaves, the child returns and continues making noise. Now consider the impact both of these "performers" have on a passing audience. Most who would stop to listen to the pianist will continue walking as the child makes noise. If you want to draw people who appreciate music, you will invite a musician who plays the instrument well. If you don't care who you draw, you'll let anyone bang away.

Think of your mind and its faculties as you would think of the piano. When your self-image is at the keyboard, you get one type of result. When your soul is at the keyboard, you get something very different. Is prayer always answered? In one sense, this is like asking if sound always comes from the piano when the keys are pressed. If the kind of sound you want is not coming from the piano, the remedy is to change the player, not get another piano.

In its highest practice, prayer begins with meditation. Think of this as bringing your soul to the keyboard and presenting its repertoire of music. As beautiful music does, this experience inspires the visual aspect of the imagination with the pure peace of knowing itself as complete, Emerson's "... *soliloquy of a beholding and jubilant soul ... the spirit of God pronouncing his works good.*" This step is the key to understanding Jesus' statement of believing you have already received the thing you are praying for. We turn our focus from the particulars of a problem, step into the concert hall of the soul, and bask in the beauty of the music. From this vantage point, we easily direct our faith to the perfect outworking of whatever our temporal problem may be. Our faculty of judgment embraces and entertains only that which is true of the soul. We exercise our will to keep our faith and imagination focused on expecting the highest outworking, even when appearances seem contrary to this expectation. Through our power of elimination, we let go of all doubt, all fear, and all feelings of uncertainty concerning circumstances.

You can see that this prayer is not a single act of putting in a request to God for some desire. You utilize this mindset all day long. Starting with an experience of the soul sets the tone. Many have created a dependence on inspiring passages from a book or the comforting word of another for their assurance that things are going to work out. These, of course, have their place. But in comparison to actually hearing the soul's music, this would be similar to studying the printed program of the concert. Meditation exposes you to the experience of *knowing*, not simply believing based on the assurance of another, that this is true. Faith centered in knowing is much more powerful than belief-dependent faith. It is the difference between hearing beautiful music and hoping someone will show up and start playing something you like.

The Prayer for Guidance

We all have moments of uncertainty, of not knowing if we are making right choices. It is easy, reading the tea leaves of circumstances, to jump to actions that, in the end, do not work out well. This is usually because we are acting from the promptings of the self-image rather than basing our decisions on what we are learning is true of our soul. The process of soul searching, then, is one of considering whether our thinking rises from the strength of our soul, or if we are searching for the best way to protect some weakness of our self-image.

Seeking guidance doesn't always begin with the apparent issue. As we will see with all of these illustrations, ideally we start with an experience of the soul. If you've ever worked a jigsaw puzzle, all the pieces spread out on a table can be daunting. It helps to look at the completed picture on the box to see what the puzzle will look like once all the pieces are in place. There will still be trial and error but you have the assurance and the confidence to forge ahead knowing that the picture you are trying to form does exist. Experiencing your soul gives you a similar larger picture. It is easier to fit the pieces of your life together coming from the strength of your soul.

Imagination

Begin with a heightened awareness of your spiritual essence, your soul, with Exercise #8, *A Full Meditation*, from the previous chapter. This meditation opens the intuitive side of your imagination, which will serve as the starting point for all the following exercises in prayer.

Once you establish a level of spiritual awareness, turn your attention to the idea of guidance. Visualize yourself as receiving guidance right now. You do this by considering how you would feel if this was true, and you open yourself to accepting it as true. Feel the freedom and complete peace of knowing the guidance you seek is now in play. You are lifting your spiritual eyes to see that which you are asking for in prayer is already yours. Release all negative imagery and energy with the following denial:

Denial

I now release all negative imagery concerning my life condition. I release all fear, all stress, all need to find a way out of this situation.

Spend a few moments letting go. As you experience a measure of freedom, speak the following words and let yourself experience the truth you are declaring:

Affirmation

The guidance I seek is now established in my life. I experience the peace of freedom knowing I am now being guided to the best and highest possible outworking of this situation. Thank You, God.

Faith

The experience described in this affirmation is now the focus of your faith, your expectation. As ideas and situations present themselves through your day, your faith in the truth of this affirmation will be challenged. It is not unusual for things to begin falling apart before they come together. If a structure rests on a faulty foundation, it is necessary to start over by replacing that foundation.

Judgment

It is here that your faculty of judgment plays an important role. When things appear to be falling apart it is easy to lose faith in the notion that better conditions are unfolding. Bear in mind that these better conditions may not look like the conditions you assume are needed to fulfill your expectations. Is your faith in specific conditions or is it in the greater good now unfolding? Do not judge by appearances.

Will

Assert your will to stay the course. This does not mean that you force yourself to believe something that runs counter to what you think is true. Think of your will as a willingness to allow this or something better to emerge. Allowing is not the same as forcing. Keep the steady attitude that your vision of greater good or something better is emerging.

Elimination

Usually when we have a concern, we run it as an endless loop mental scenario that leads to nothing good. If you waver in your conviction to hold to the best and highest, as you surely will, re-gather your spiritual wits and release the temptation to let appearances dictate this negative mental movie. Utilize the above denial and affirmation to release and refocus.

Prayer for Healing

Embracing the soul as complete and expressing first as a whole, spiritual body is a very powerful healing image. This helps us remember that our body serves our soul as the interfacing agent to the material world. It is easy to let the body become our center of attention both in times of wellness and in times of sickness. For most of us, the body has become like a dog on a leash, pulling us in the direction of its choice. We no longer walk the dog; the dog is walking us.

Our prayer for healing is as much about regaining the perspective of bodily mastery as it is about healing the body. When pain is involved, this change of attitude will be difficult. But you must remember that your highest reason for being on this planet and in this body does not include making your body the total focus of your attention in ways that keeps you rushing to fill its every need. Your body is here to serve you, not the other way around.

As with guidance, seeking healing never begins with the body's present condition. Healing begins by raising our perspective, remembering that we are a soul with a body and that our soul is now complete and radiating wholeness

Imagination

Once you establish a level of spiritual awareness through your meditative process, bring into the field of your awareness the notion of healing. Hold the image of your soul as a great central light radiating throughout your body as perfect wholeness. Get a clear feeling that you are this radiating light and you are blessing your body with your healing radiance. This healing is not happening to you. This healing is you. You are agreeing to impart your healing essence to and through your body.

Denial

I now release the belief that I am my body. I release the energy of restriction imposed by my body. I am not here to serve my body. My body is here to serve me.

Affirmation

My body joyously responds in service to my soul. My soul's freedom and completeness expresses as beauty of mind, body, and affairs. My body is my loving and faithful servant, and it performs its service in great joy.

Faith

Your faculty of faith is grounded in the truth that you are your soul, a whole spiritual being expressing through this physical body.

Judgment

Perhaps pain, a doctor's report, or some other body-based information will cause you to waver from your soul-centered healing process. This information and the thinking it inspires has nothing to do with the truth of your complete soul. You are under no obligation to define yourself by pain or restriction in your body. Exercise your spiritual judgment by saying, *This is not me. This is not who or what I am.*

Will

When Jesus asked the man by the sheep gate if he wanted to be healed, he was asking him if he was willing to stop running the scenario that kept him lying helpless by the pool. Was he willing to change that scenario? Become willing to keep your imagination and your faith centered on your wholeness. You are a complete soul expressing through this physical body. It is the will of your soul to be free and your body is responding beautifully.

Elimination

Let go of all imagery and all emotion concerning perceived restrictions imposed by your body. You are perpetually free now. There are no restrictions imposed on your soul.

Prayer for Prosperity

A good starting point concerning prosperity is the realization that your soul is already complete. There is nothing found at the material level to make you any more complete than you are now. Because of our life-long habit of catering to the self-image, it is easy to confuse the needs and desires of this false sense of self with the truth of the soul. Your soul is imbued with the fundamental intelligence of God. Like a seed planted in the ground, you inherently know how to express successfully through the material plane. Like the seed, you know how to draw from your environment the proper nutrients that allow your soul to express successfully.

All of your executive faculties are important, but those of judgment and elimination may require special attention here. Are you trying to prosper, advance, and protect a weakness of the self-image, or are you responding to the promptings of your soul? The "voice" of your soul is your innate desire for greater freedom. If you are attempting to realize this desire by forcing it into a channel concocted by your self-image, the result will be frustration and blockage at every turn.

Imagination

After establishing your awareness in the spiritual level, see your complete soul as a seed planted in your material environment drawing all the energy rich nutrients you need to fully express who and what you are at the deepest, most meaningful level.

Denial

I now release the belief in any apparent barrier to my soul's greater good. I release all fear, all discouragement, all frustration, all feelings of being trapped.

Affirmation

The divine intelligence of my soul knows how to express as complete success and freedom. I am open and receptive to new inspiration and prospering ideas that bring about right conditions for my soul's highest good.

Faith

Turn the great power of your faith to your soul with the absolute expectation that everything you need to express fully and completely in this material world is now being provided.

Judgment

Be vigilant in your discernment between the needs of your self-image and the genuine promptings of your soul. Affirm that you clearly see the difference and that your judgment is sound.

Will

Affirm your willingness to say this or something better to the prosperity issue you are considering. The will of your soul is complete freedom. Be willing to receive instruction through the greater intelligence that is asserting itself through you now. Thinking of your complete soul, affirm thy will is being done now.

Elimination

Release your investment in all preconceived outcomes. If you find yourself getting anxious, let go of these feelings and know the truth that your soul's greater good is now manifesting. If one path is blocked, release it in joy knowing another, better path is making itself clear to you now.

IN CONCLUSION

I hope you have received some benefit from reading *The Complete Soul*. For me, the most meaningful books are not those that tell us how to think, but those that confirm what we have thought and deeply felt in solitude, others have thought and felt as well. If I've conveyed some measure of this assurance, if I've confirmed something you have suspected but maybe never said aloud, then this book has accomplished half the work it was sent to do. My hope for the other half is that something within these pages has inspired you to trust the validity of your own spiritual promptings.

Regardless of how many books you read or classes you take, your self-image will never evolve into what your soul already is. Nor will your capacity to know your soul ever be any greater than it is right now. There are no natural barriers surrounding your complete soul. There is nothing preventing you from fulfilling your reason for taking on a body and experiencing life on this planet.

You and I did not come here to wander aimlessly looking for something in people, places, and things that we do not already have. Think about this. What missing piece of you could this earth possibly hold?

From the point of view of your complete soul, there is really only one possible answer. The one thing that earth holds for you is the life you intended to live when you made the choice to come here.